MW00773292

FOUND *in* TRANSLATION

LOVE אהבה

museum of the Bible
BOOKS

WORTHY®
Inspired

Table of Contents

Introduction

Many languages include words that have multiple meanings, depending on their contexts. This assortment of meanings can bring a sense of beauty, intrigue, and complexity to a language. The Hebrew language is no exception.

In the Hebrew Bible, a word or phrase can mean one thing in one passage but something entirely different in another passage. This allows for variances in interpretation and translation, which inevitably leads to challenges for Bible translators, who must often select one meaning of a Hebrew word or phrase to use in a biblical passage in an effort to best represent the word in another language. As a result, not everyone who reads a modern translation of the Bible will fully understand or appreciate the intended message communicated by the author in the original language.

Found in Translation provides readers with a unique perspective on how Hebrew words are used in the Bible. Written in short, inspirational messages, the chapters in this book explore fifty-two Hebrew words and phrases used by the original biblical authors. Definitions and contexts help to explain the significance of the Hebrew words in a way that will connect readers more deeply to the characters, stories, prayers, and insights found within the pages of the Bible.

ʾāḏām

humanity

'āḏām - אָדָם

וַיִּיצֶר יְהוָה אֱלֹהִים אֶת־הָאָדָם עָפָר מִן־הָאֲדָמָה

"Then the LORD God formed man of the dust of the ground."
Genesis 2:7

Adam (אָדָם) is much more than the proper name most English speakers associate with the biblical figure. According to Genesis 2, Adam was the first human. But his name is used as a reference for any human in the Hebrew language.

Adam can refer to a number of related identities and concepts. In Genesis 1:27, for instance, the Hebrew actually says "the *adam*" (הָאָדָם), which makes *adam* the object that is simply the created human because adding an article is not done with a proper name in Hebrew. This resists the idea of considering *Adam* to be a proper name referring to the first man. Combined with the innumerable places in which the Bible uses the word to refer to humanity more generally, *'āḏām* should likely be thought of broadly as a representative of humanity.

The word 'ādām also has a substantial connection to the word for "earth" or "ground" in Hebrew—'ādāmāh (אֲדָמָה). To many people who read the Bible, this is often justified by noting that Adam, who was created from

'ādām

אָדָם

"humanity"

Adam, the proper name
—Genesis 5:2

The first human
—Genesis 2:7

A human, anyone
—Leviticus 1:2

the earth, "became a living soul" after God "breathed into his nostrils the breath of life" (Genesis 2:7). However, the relationship between the words is deeper, and this is demonstrated by a preceding verse. Genesis 2:5 states, "No shrub of the field was yet in the earth, and no herb of the field had yet sprung up; for the LORD God had not caused it to rain upon the earth, and there was not a man to till the ground." In this verse, the Hebrew spellings of the words for *human* and *ground* are almost identical.

Genesis 2:5 establishes that no plants grew because God had not yet given rain and there were no humans to work the soil. The next two verses show God first giving water to the land (2:6) and then forming man (2:7). Genesis 2:15 says, "The LORD God took the man and put him in the garden of Eden to work it and keep it" (ESV). Many Bible scholars would conclude, based on these verses in Genesis 2, that one of God's intended purposes for humanity is to "work," or "till," the earth.

Another profound connection between the Hebrew words for *man* and *ground* can be found in Adam's punishment for eating the fruit from the tree of the knowledge of good and evil (Genesis 2:15–17, 3:6). God says to Adam in Genesis 3:17, "Because you have listened to the voice of your wife and have eaten of the tree of which I commanded you, 'You shall not eat of it,' cursed is the ground because of you; in pain you shall eat of it all the days of your life' " (ESV). This punishment, or curse, is often associated with why humanity is forced to work the earth. From the verses in Genesis 2–3, it appears that God intended for humanity ('āḏām) to work the ground as a pleasurable duty; the work, however, became a laborious chore as a punishment for disobedience.

If we reflect on God's original intentions regarding work for Adam, based on Genesis 2, how might that change our own views and attitudes about our work?

אָדָם

7

אַהֲבָה

ʾahăbāh

love

'ahăbāh - אַהֲבָה

וְאָהַבְתָּ אֵת יְהוָה אֱלֹהֶיךָ בְּכָל־לְבָבְךָ
וּבְכָל־נַפְשְׁךָ וּבְכָל־מְאֹדֶךָ

*"And thou shalt love the LORD thy God with all thy heart,
and with all thy soul, and with all thy might."*
Deuteronomy 6:5

Many people question the nature of love. The Bible provides us with compelling insights about this question. In Deuteronomy 6:5, for example, God commands the people of Israel to love him. The Hebrew word for *love* (*'ahăbāh* אַהֲבָה) in this verse implies a willingness to give one's whole being in service to God.

Jewish commentator Rashi (1040–1105) pointed out that there is a difference between a person's love for God and their love for another human being.[1] He explained that serving God is a much better way to love him than loving him because of fear. While fear can inspire obedience, love is a far superior motive.

Twentieth-century rabbi Eliyahu Dessler compared the similar Hebrew words for "to love" (*'ahăbāh*) and "to give" (*yāhab*).[2] In his comparison, he suggested the meaning of love is linked to generosity—it involves giving rather than taking. Based on this connection, love contributes to the good of another, even when that commitment involves personal sacrifice.

Rabbi Akiva (AD 50–135) explains in the Talmud (*Brachot* 61b) that "[to give] with all your soul is being willing to even sacrifice your soul." A prime example of this kind of sacrifice can be seen in 1 Samuel 18:1: "As soon as he had finished speaking to Saul, the soul of Jonathan was knit to the soul of David, and Jonathan loved him as his own soul" (ESV). This verse describes Jonathan's soul as being connected—"knit"—to David's soul. Jonathan loved David as himself. They loved each other so much they were like one soul. In the Jewish tradition, this is the highest form of love, where people care about each other as they care for themselves. It is also the opposite of hate, where people wish bad things on somebody else. In this context, *'ahăbāh*—true love—means caring about another person without expecting anything in return. That is true selflessness.

'ahăbāh

אַהֲבָה

"love"

A human's love for another human
—Psalm 109:4

God's love for Israel
—Hosea 11:4

Carnal love
—2 Samuel 13:15

This type of love, demonstrated by sacrificial giving to one another, often engenders deep and lasting affection. It can be a way of inspiring more giving, which helps promote a virtuous cycle of love.

By understanding the Hebrew word *'ahăḇāh*, we have an opportunity to reflect on how we view the command in Deuteronomy 6:5: "You shall love the LORD your God with all your heart and with all your soul and with all your might" (ESV). The Hebrew indicates that loving God involves a willingness to give of ourselves in active love.

אַהֲבָה

אַלְמָנָה וְיָתוֹם

ʾalmānāh wəyāṯôm

widow and orphan

'almānāh wəyāṯôm - אַלְמָנָה וְיָתוֹם

כָּל־אַלְמָנָה וְיָתוֹם לֹא תְעַנּוּן אִם עַנֵּה
תְעַנֶּה אֹתוֹ....... וְחָרָה אַפִּי וְהָרַגְתִּי
אֶתְכֶם בֶּחָרֶב וְהָיוּ נְשֵׁיכֶם אַלְמָנוֹת
וּבְנֵיכֶם יְתֹמִים

"Ye shall not afflict any widow, or fatherless child.
If thou afflict them in any wise . . . My wrath shall wax hot,
and I will kill you with the sword; and your wives shall be
widows, and your children fatherless."
Exodus 22:21–23 [3]

Exodus 22:21–23 conveys God's love for widows and orphans. In fact, the two Hebrew words *'almānāh wəyāṯôm* (אַלְמָנָה וְיָתוֹם)—"widow and orphan"—appear together frequently in the Bible (around thirty times).

Importantly, the phrase "widow and orphan" is often positioned in the Bible in a series of commandments where

13

God is concerned with protecting several vulnerable populations who suffer hardship or oppression. Exodus chapters 21–23 describe such vulnerable populations as second wives (21:10), pregnant women (21:22–23), slaves (21:26–27), virgins (22:16–17), the poor (22:25), and im-

'almānāh wəyāṯôm

אַלְמָנָה וְיָתוֹם

"widow and orphan"

Vulnerable
—Exodus 22:21–23

Shamed/Disgraced
—Isaiah 54:4

Destitute
—Lamentations 1:1

migrants (22:21, 23:9). But widows and orphans (*'almānāh wəyāṯôm*) stand out as the prototypical examples of vulnerable groups. The earlier literature from the Canaanites emphasized taking care of these two groups, as did the later literature of the New Testament, which defines "pure" religion as this: "to visit orphans and widows in their affliction" (James 1:27, ESV).

These two Hebrew words are ancient in the language and seem to have no identifiable roots. What characterizes both groups and makes them so vulnerable is their isolated nature in ancient society. With the death of her husband, the widow stood alone, the societal norms preventing her from conducting even the most mundane of business transactions without him. Similarly, in a time before even the imperfect models of the orphanage and foster homes, children who lost their parents were entirely at the mercy of the kindness of strangers and distant relatives. Fittingly, the words themselves are left floating alone, without a strong anchor in the language.

On rare occasions, the term *widow* (*'almānāh*) is also used as a metaphor in the Bible for the spiritual condition of a nation or culture. For example, the author of the book of Lamentations refers to Jerusalem as a "widow" during the Babylonian exile: "How lonely sits the city that was full of people! How like a widow [*'almānāh*] has she become, she who was great among the nations!" (1:1, ESV; see also Isaiah 54:3–5). But most uses of the phrase "widow and orphan" (*'almānāh wəyāṯôm*) in the Hebrew Bible contain commands to care for the needs of actual orphans and widows.

Perhaps the biblical emphasis on caring for the fatherless and widows can inspire us to find ways to bring relief to vulnerable people around the world.

אַלְמָנָה
וְיָתוֹם

ʾăšērāh

a tree planted for idolatrous purposes

אֲשֵׁרָה - 'ăšērāh

לֹא תִטַּע לְךָ אֲשֵׁרָה כָּל עֵץ אֵצֶל
מִזְבַּח יְהוָֹה אֱלֹהֶיךָ אֲשֶׁר תַּעֲשֶׂה לָּךְ

"Thou shalt not plant thee an Asherah of any
kind of tree beside the altar of the LORD thy God,
which thou shalt make thee."
Deuteronomy 16:21

In life, some choices might appear good on the surface, when in fact they lead to tragic consequences. Proverbs 14:12 says, "There is a way that seems right to a man, but its end is the way to death" (ESV).

This principle is conveyed in the subtleties of the Hebrew word *'ăšērāh* (אֲשֵׁרָה). The first appearance of this word in the Bible is in Deuteronomy 16:21. Historical research shows that *'ăšērôṭ* (the plural of *'ăšērāh*) are images of an indigenous mother goddess dating back to the Hittites and Sumerians. The Mishnah (*Avodah Zarah* 3:6–7), however, defines an *'ăšērāh* in three ways: (1) a tree that has been planted for

17

purposes of idolatry, (2) a tree that has been pruned for idolatrous purposes, or (3) a tree that has an idol planted beneath it.

In numerous biblical references, we see the Israelites struggling to ban and destroy the *'ăšērôṯ* that are so common in the nations surrounding them. For example, in 2 Kings 23:4–6, young king Josiah sets out to completely destroy the items used for idol worship that had accumulated in God's temple. "He brought out the Asherah from the house of the Lord . . . and burned it at the brook Kidron and beat it to dust" (verse 6, ESV).

In Hebrew, the two words that form the word *'ăšērāh* carry an illusion of potentially being a good thing. These two words have only slight differences in their vowels. The verb יָשַׁר (*yāšar*) means "to straighten" or "to direct," and the word אָשֵּׁר (*'iššar*) means "to be happy." Combined, the pair sounds like the related word *'ăšērāh*.

Nachmanides points out that the term *'ăšērāh* might well be related to the words "my steps" אֲשֻׁרַי (*'ăšuray*) used in Psalm 17:5.[4] An *'ăšērāh* would be planted next to a pagan altar to show the pagan way. So, we can imagine how someone might believe that *'ăšērôṯ* are positive things to have around. Indeed, what could be wrong with moral correctness and happiness?

'ăšērāh

אֲשֵׁרָה

"a tree planted for idolatrous purposes"

The goddess
—2 Kings 23:4

The idol
—1 Kings 16:33

The tree
—Deuteronomy 16:21

However, in 2 Kings 21:2–7, we see a list of evils promoted by Manasseh, one of Judah's kings, who commits "much evil in the sight of the LORD, provoking him to anger" (verse 6, ESV). He rebuilds mountain altars (called "high places"), constructs new altars for the god Baal, worships stars and planets, practices soothsaying and divination, burns one of his own sons as an offering to idols, and places "a carved image of Asherah" in the temple in Jerusalem. In this context the "image of Asherah" was a four-cornered idol (as opposed to God's throne that is described in Ezekiel) with four forms: an insect, a fish, a bird, and an animal. It is probably referred to as an "image of Asherah" because it had been placed in the temple, like an *'ăšērāh*.

While the root words used to form *'ăšērāh* carry positive surface connotations, 2 Kings 21 clearly includes *'ăšērāh* as being one expression of Manasseh's many evil practices. In Deuteronomy 16:21, the Israelites are told to avoid this idol, but it persists in some of their religious practices for generations.

The contrast between what an *'ăšērāh* appears to be on the surface and what it actually is can provide us with a helpful warning. Perhaps we can learn from the story of the *'ăšērāh* that what might at first seem good to us can lead us down terrible paths.

אֲשֵׁרָה

עַבְדַי

הַנְּבִיאִם

ʿăḇāḏay hannəḇîʾîm

my servants the prophets

ʿăḇāḏay hannəḇîʾîm - עֲבָדַי הַנְּבִיאִים

שֻׁבוּ מִדַּרְכֵיכֶם הָרָעִים וְשִׁמְרוּ מִצְוֹתַי

חֻקּוֹתַי כְּכָל־הַתּוֹרָה אֲשֶׁר צִוִּיתִי

אֶת־אֲבֹתֵיכֶם וַאֲשֶׁר שָׁלַחְתִּי אֲלֵיכֶם

בְּיַד עֲבָדַי הַנְּבִיאִים

*"Turn ye from your evil ways, and keep My commandments
and My statutes, according to all the law which I
commanded your fathers, and which I sent to you
by the hand of My servants the prophets."*
2 Kings 17:13

You might know someone who is a centenarian. In the course of their lifetimes these remarkable people have seen the world go from horse and buggy to moon landings and space shuttles. They used to send handwritten letters that took weeks to arrive in the mail, and now they can send emails and texts that arrive in seconds. This astounding pace of change in modern life can leave even young people feeling as though nothing is stable or permanent.

In the Jewish tradition, the phrase "My servants the prophets," which in Hebrew is ʿăḇāḏay hannəḇîʾîm (עֲבָדַי הַנְּבִיאִים),

21

is a reminder of God's steadfast, unchanging truth. This phrase is found throughout the Hebrew Bible (2 Kings 9:7; Jeremiah 7:25, 26:5, 29:19, 35:15, 44:4; Ezekiel 38:17; Zechariah 1:6) and can indicate that the biblical writers viewed the words God spoke to the prophets as a source of stability in life.

ʿăḇāḏay hannəḇîʾîm

עֲבָדַי הַנְּבִיאִים

"my servants the prophets"

The prophets
—2 Kings 17:13

Israel's true ancestors
—Zechariah 1:6

Emissaries for God
—Jeremiah 7:25

In 2 Kings 17:13 God commands the people of Israel to keep his law just as he commanded their ancestors to keep it. The Hebrew phrase *ʿăḇāḏay hannəḇîʾîm* connects the Israelites' ancestors and the prophets in an important way. The prophet Zechariah elaborates on this connection. He says in Zechariah 1:5–6: "Your fathers, where are they? And the prophets, do they live forever? But my words and my statutes, which I commanded my servants the prophets, did they not overtake your fathers? So they repented and said, 'As the LORD of hosts purposed to deal with us for our ways and deeds, so has he dealt with us' " (ESV).

The word *ʿeḇeḏ haššēm* (עֶבֶד יְהוָה) means "a servant of the Lord." Abraham (Genesis 26:24), the Israelites (Leviticus 25:42), and Moses (Numbers 12:7) are all described as God's servants. In these contexts, the word refers to people who devote themselves to serving God. The word *ʿeḇeḏ* can also mean "a slave" (Deuteronomy 6:21) or "a servant" (Exodus 10:7). A derivative form, *'ăḇōḏāh*, means either "work" or "slavery" (Exodus 1:14). In the *Hiphil* (causative) conjugation, this means "to enslave" (Exodus 1:13).

As seen throughout the Hebrew Bible, from the time when God gave the Israelites the law to the time of the later prophets, the people often turned away from God. Jeremiah 7:25–26 says, "From the day that your fathers came out of the land of Egypt to this day, I have persistently sent all my servants the prophets to them, day after day. Yet they did not listen to me or incline their ear, but stiffened their neck. They did worse than their fathers" (ESV). According to these verses, God persisted in sending the prophets to the people.

These verses from Zechariah suggest that God's words and statutes given to the prophets led the previous generations of Israelites to repent from their wrongdoing. This indicates Zechariah's belief that each generation of Israelites is held accountable according to the standard of God's words that were declared by the prophets before them. This, in Jewish tradition, is why so many biblical verses include the phrase "my servants the prophets."

The verses from 2 Kings 17:13, Jeremiah 7:25–26, and Zechariah 1:5–6 show that God's standards—his commands and laws—transcend generational changes within the biblical framework. Many people who seek wisdom and truth from the Bible view the words within it as a consistent message from God, whose standards remain constant and are not distorted by generations of rapid technological, economic, and social change.

עַבְדַּי
הַנְּבִיאִים

עַבְדִּי

ʿaḇdî

my servant

עַבְדִּי - ʻabdî

נְבוּכַדְרֶאצַּר מֶלֶךְ בָּבֶל עַבְדִּי

"Nebuchadrezzar the king of Babylon, My servant."
Jeremiah 25:9

I n Jeremiah 25:9, God calls Nebuchadrezzar (more commonly known as Nebuchadnezzar), king of Babylon, "My servant." This might seem odd to many, because later in the chapter, God says this king will be punished for his "iniquity" (Jeremiah 25:12). Why would God call such a king his "servant"?

This is no idle question for the Israelites living during the reign of Nebuchadnezzar. Imagine yourself as a person living in Judah at the time when the Babylonians, under orders of King Nebuchadnezzar, invade your homeland, destroy your sacred temple, and force you and your entire community into exile under foreign rule. Then, imagine that God says that the king who conquered your nation is his "servant." You would understandably be shocked and confused.

25

And yet, in Jeremiah 25:8–9, that is what God calls the Babylonian king:

Therefore thus saith the LORD of hosts: Because ye have not heard My words, behold, I will send and take all the families of the north, saith the LORD, and I will send unto Nebuchadrezzar the king of Babylon, My servant, and will bring them against this land, and against the inhabitants thereof, and against all these nations round about; and I will utterly destroy them, and make them an astonishment, and a hissing, and perpetual desolations.

The Hebrew in this passage corresponding to "servant" is ʾăḇdî (עַבְדִּי), and it literally means "my servant" or "my slave." In both English and Hebrew, a servant (ʾeḇeḏ) is a person who does work for someone else. The Hebrew meaning simply indicates that God is using Nebuchadnezzar to accomplish God's purposes. In this one Hebrew word, ʾăḇdî, we perhaps find a profound biblical claim that even in perplexing circumstances, God is working.

According to the biblical narrative, what the people of Judah endure in Jeremiah's time is catastrophic. They are killed or led into exile, forced to live under foreign rule. We can all recognize that having your homeland destroyed must have been horrific. And yet, amid

ʾăḇdî

עַבְדִּי

"my servant"

Slave (permanent property)
—Deuteronomy 25:15
(25:16 Heb)

Servant (temporary employee)
—Genesis 40:20

*Advisor/official
(political/military subordinate)*
—2 Kings 22:12

tragic circumstances, Jeremiah claims that God is fulfilling his purposes by using Nebuchadnezzar as his servant.

This story in Jeremiah could provide a hopeful perspective on questions about the goodness of God in the midst of suffering. One possible response to suffering, as shown in Jeremiah 25, is to trust in the sovereignty of God. In practice, this kind of faith helps many people go through times of suffering with hope and courage.

עַבְדִּי

בַּעַל

ba'al

master

ba'al - בַּעַל

וְהָיָה בַיּוֹם־הַהוּא נְאֻם־יְהוָה תִּקְרְאִי
אִישִׁי וְלֹא־תִקְרְאִי־לִי עוֹד בַּעְלִי

*"And it shall be at that day, saith the LORD, that thou shalt call
Me 'îšî [Husband], and shalt call Me no more Baʿălî [Baʿal]."*
Hosea 2:16 [5]

The book of Hosea is primarily about God calling the people of Israel out of idolatry and back into a sincere relationship with him. Hosea 4:1–2 summarizes the situation in Israel during this time: "There is no faithfulness or steadfast love, and no knowledge of God in the land; there is swearing, lying, murder, stealing, and committing adultery; they break all bounds, and bloodshed follows bloodshed" (ESV).

In that dismal context, Hosea 2:16 says, "And in that day, declares the LORD, you will call me 'My Husband,' and no longer will you call me 'My Baal' " (ESV). In this statement, God expresses his desire to treat even those who have turned from him as a loving husband would treat a wife.

The Hebrew word *ba'al* (בַּעַל) usually means "master" and conveys an element of ownership. *Ba'al* can refer to "the owner of something" (however, a different word, *'āḏôn*, is used for a "slave owner"). A *ba'al habbayit*, for example,

ba'al

בַּעַל

"master"

Possessor or owner
—Exodus 21:34, 22:7, 10;
Isaiah 1:3

Husband
—Exodus 21:22;
2 Samuel 11:26

A deity other than the God of Israel
—Judges 6:25–32;
Hosea 2:16–17

means "the master of the house" and refers to a landlord. *Ba'al hassəpînāh* means "a boat owner." The term *ba'al* is also used figuratively, such as in the expression *ba'al hakkəṯaḇ*, which means "the owner of the writing" (an author). *Ba'al* can also mean "husband" (Deuteronomy 24:4) or "to have intercourse" (Deuteronomy 24:1).

The type of ownership conveyed in Hosea 2:16 is the idea of a child belonging to a parent, or of a husband and wife belonging to each other, in a caring and protective manner. In this verse, God says his people will call him *'îšî* ("my man") and not *Ba'alî* ("my master"). The lowercase letter *i* at the ends of the words *'îšî* and *Ba'alî* means "my." In relation to the word *'îšî*, this letter conveys the type of loving ownership that we find in intimate relationships, such as a marriage. The idea is expressed when a husband says, "This is *my* wife," or when a wife says, "This is *my* husband."

By studying the meaning of this one letter at the end of

each Hebrew word, we can see that God expresses through these words in the Bible that he does not want to be called "my ba'al" ("my master") but "my 'îš" ("my man"). This is the beautiful sentiment that God expresses to Israel in Hosea. Understanding these words helps us see in the book of Hosea that God desires a loving relationship in which people belong to him.

בַּעַל

בָּחַר

bāḥar

to choose

bāḥar - בָּחַר

וְהָיָה הַמָּקוֹם אֲשֶׁר־יִבְחַר יְהוָה
אֱלֹהֵיכֶם בּוֹ לְשַׁכֵּן שְׁמוֹ שָׁם שָׁמָּה
תָבִיאוּ אֵת כָּל־אֲשֶׁר אָנֹכִי מְצַוֶּה אֶתְכֶם

"Then it shall come to pass that the place which the LORD your God shall choose to cause His name to dwell there, thither shall ye bring all that I command you."
Deuteronomy 12:11

When reading the Bible, people sometimes encounter an apparent contradiction and then decide to either disbelieve what is written or to leave the question dormant.

This point can be seen in an apparent contradiction surrounding the Hebrew word for "shall choose" or "will choose" (*yibḥar* יִבְחַר). This is the same word that is used to say that Israel is God's chosen people and "treasured possession" in Deuteronomy 7:6 (ESV). The word conveys the

33

idea that God is not simply picking a nice location for the people of Israel; he is choosing Israel with love such as that of a couple adopting a child.

The same word, *yibḥar*, is used again in reference to the time before the Israelites cross the Jordan into Israel. Moses says to the Israelites that God will give them rest from their enemies and "shall choose" a place for his "name to dwell" (Deuteronomy 12:10–11).

However, these verses in Deuteronomy 12, which say that God will choose a place for his dwelling, seem to contradict what is stated in 1 Kings 8:16. Here God (quoted by Solomon) says, "Since the day that I brought my people Israel out of Egypt, I chose no city out of all the tribes of Israel in which to build a house, that my name might be there. But I chose David to be over my people Israel" (ESV). Solomon follows those words by saying, "Now it was in the heart of David my father to build a house for the name of the LORD, the God of Israel" (1 Kings 8:17, ESV).

This apparent contradiction—seen in the words "I chose no city"—can actually be seen as revealing a profound aspect of God's nature. Although people of many religions establish specific sites for their gods, such as Athena being the patron-god of Athens,

bāḥar

בָּחַר

"to choose"

Choose
—Deuteronomy 7:6

Select
—Deuteronomy 12:10–11

Reveal preference
—1 Kings 8:16

God (according to Deuteronomy 12) chooses where he wants his temple to be built. Some Bible scholars explain the words in 1 Kings 8:16–17 to mean that God does not reveal where he has chosen his house to be built until David is chosen as king over Israel, and then God places the building of his temple in the heart of David and the hands of Solomon. It's possible to conclude that God is seeking a person who can understand what it means to be chosen in a relationship with him.

This example shows us that by careful study of apparent contradictions in the Bible, we are often able to mine deeper meanings and truths from our inquiries than if we simply leave our questions unattended.

בָּחַר

בָּמָה

bāmāh

high place

bāmāh - בָּמָה

וַיְחַפְּאוּ בְנֵי־יִשְׂרָאֵל דְּבָרִים אֲשֶׁר לֹא־כֵן
עַל־יְהוָה אֱלֹהֵיהֶם וַיִּבְנוּ לָהֶם בָּמוֹת
בְּכָל־עָרֵיהֶם מִמִּגְדַּל נוֹצְרִים עַד־עִיר מִבְצָר

"The children of Israel did impute things that were not right
unto the LORD their God, and they built them high places in all
their cities, from the tower of the watchmen to the fortified city."
2 Kings 17:9

I f we read through the books of 1 and 2 Kings and look for references to "high places," we can begin to see something that could be compared to a disease that is extremely difficult to eradicate.

A "high place," or *bāmāh* (בָּמָה), is a location mentioned in the Bible where idolatrous sacrifices often took place. According to Numbers 33:52, God had ordered the people of Israel to destroy "all their high places." These high places and sacrifices appear to originate from the polytheistic cultures

37

that surrounded Israel, according to the biblical narrative. At times, the use of high places seeped into Israel's religious practices.

It's possible that a compromise by King Solomon opened the door to more serious problems with high places later in the biblical narrative of Israel's

history: "Solomon loved the LORD, walking in the statutes of David his father, *only he sacrificed and made offerings at the high places*" (1 Kings 3:3, ESV, emphasis added). During Solomon's reign, the Israelites offer sacrifices at the high places because the temple has not yet been constructed (1 Kings 3:2). Solomon also offers 1,000 burnt offerings on the *bāmāh* in Gibeon the night before having the dream of God granting him wisdom (1 Kings 3:2–5).

From that point forward, we find a litany of Israel's kings who either blatantly promote idolatry at the high places or try to do what is right in God's eyes but fail to eradicate all the idolatrous practices and constructions, including the high places. To name a few these kings: Jeroboam (1 Kings 12:32); Jehoshaphat (1 Kings 22:43); Jehoash (2 Kings 12:2–4); Amaziah (2 Kings 14:1–4); and Ahaz (2 Kings 16:4).

The problem became so entrenched over time that in 2 Kings 17 we learn that God allows the Assyrians to invade and carry "the Israelites away to Assyria" (verse 6, ESV). This chapter also provides the specific reasons why God allowed this to occur: The people of Israel "feared other gods and walked in the customs of the nations" (verses 7–8, ESV); the people acted immorally, attempting to hide wrongdoing from God (verse 9); "they built for themselves high places in all their towns" (verse 9, ESV); and they made idolatrous "offerings on all the high places" (verse 11, ESV).

Looking at this overview, it's possible to conclude that despite the repeated warnings of prophets (2 Kings 17:13) and the efforts of good kings, the high places and other forms of idolatry persisted, thereby entangling the nation of Israel in practices that God abhors.

In the book of Ezekiel, God describes the high places using a Hebrew play on words: "What is the high place to which you go? So its name is called Bamah to this day" (20:29, ESV). The word for *what* in Hebrew is *māh*. For instance, *lāmāh* means "For what?" or "Why?" In this verse, Ezekiel is making fun of idolaters who call their altar a "Bamah." In the Hebrew tradition, this term is reserved for places that angels or holy personages such as Elijah might come down from heaven to visit. It is not an appropriate term for an altar used for idol worship.

Thinking carefully about the word *bamah* in the biblical context of Israel's history, we might find an opportunity to evaluate our present-day cultures to see if there are modern-day "high places" and what impact they might have in our lives.

בָּמָה

39

בַּיִת

bayit

home

בַּיִת - bayit

וְהִקְרִיב אַהֲרֹן אֶת־פַּר הַחַטָּאת
אֲשֶׁר־לוֹ וְכִפֶּר בַּעֲדוֹ וּבְעַד בֵּיתוֹ

*"And Aaron shall present the bullock of the
sin-offering, which is for himself, and make atonement for
himself, and for his house."*
Leviticus 16:6

A ny parent who has sent grown children to college
knows how difficult it can be to release sons and
daughters into the unknown. Nevertheless, most parents
recognize that young men and women must step into their
own adventures, make their own decisions, and test their
own limits.

In Genesis 2:24, there is an indication that this pattern is
central to God's design for life: "Therefore a man shall leave
his father and his mother and hold fast to his wife, and they
shall become one flesh" (ESV). The process here is for grown
children to leave the parents' household and form a new
home for a new generation.

In Hebrew, the word for *home* is *bayit* (בַּיִת). Based on

41

the Hebrew terminology, we see that at the deepest level, home is the family. As grown children leave the "nest," they are perhaps better able to face the challenges ahead because they have the support and safety of the home. They don't stay home, but home is there for them.

The word *bayiṭ* has many connotations. It can refer to a house, a home, a dynasty, or even a particular group. We see *bayiṭ* referred to as a "house" in Exodus 12:30, and as a dynasty in Exodus 1:21. *Bayiṭ* is referred to as a home in Esther 7:8. Within the Bible, *bayiṭ* also refers to the priesthood, as we see in Leviticus 16:6 (see also Leviticus 16:17, Psalms 118:3, 135:19).

The Hebrew language also takes us into a deeper understanding of another element of the home: the nature of marriage. Proverbs 31 portrays a courageous woman who is described as "a woman who fears the LORD" (verse 30, ESV). This passage is recited as a blessing by Jewish husbands for their wives every week on the Sabbath. It is a Jewish tribute for a wife, as she is seen as being entrusted with her husband's heart. "An excellent wife who can find? She is far more precious than jewels. The heart of her husband trusts in her, and he will have no lack of gain" (Proverbs 31:10–11, ESV).

bayiṭ

בַּיִת

"home"

House
—Exodus 12:30

Dynasty/Family line
—Exodus 1:21

The home/place of a certain thing
—Esther 7:8

As we reflect on this profound Hebrew word for *home*, we can consider how to develop and nurture the home that *is* the family.

בַּיִת

בְּכָל־לְבָבְךָ

וּבְכָל־נַפְשֶׁךָ

bəḵol-ləḇāḇḵā ûḇəḵol-napšəḵā

with all your heart and with all your soul

bəkol-ləbābkā
ûbəkol-napšəkā -

בְּכָל־לְבָבְךָ וּבְכָל־נַפְשֶׁךָ

וּלְאַהֲבָה אֹתוֹ וְלַעֲבֹד אֶת־יְהוָה
אֱלֹהֶיךָ בְּכָל־לְבָבְךָ וּבְכָל־נַפְשֶׁךָ

"And now, Israel, what doth the LORD thy God require
of thee, but to fear the LORD thy God, to walk in
all His ways, and to love him, and to serve the LORD thy God
with all thy heart and with all thy soul."
Deuteronomy 10:12

With all thy heart and with all thy soul." The Hebrew language displays the beauty of this phrase in ways the English version can miss. The Hebrew aligns two well-chosen words with a preposition to unveil a deep meaning.

The word *lēbāb* (לְבָב) carries a similar meaning to the

English use of the word *heart.* *Heart* is usually used in the Bible to refer to a person's innermost self. There is little difference between the English and Hebrew concepts. Perhaps this speaks to how fundamental the heart is to the human psyche. Interestingly, the usual word used for *heart* in

bəkol-ləbābkā
ûbəkol-napšəkā

בְּכָל־לְבָבְךָ וּבְכָל־נַפְשְׁךָ

"with all your heart and with all your soul"

To make permanent
—Deuteronomy 6:5

Loving worship of God
—Deuteronomy 10:12

Animating force
—Genesis 2:7

Hebrew is *lēb* (לֵב), not the *lēbāb* form used in Deuteronomy 10:12. This poetic form, *lēbāb*, is also found elsewhere (see Deuteronomy 4:29, 6:5, 20:8, 28:47, 30:6).

Lēbābkā is a possessive form and has a possessive suffix that means "your." So *lēbāb* means "a heart," whereas *lēbābkā* means "your heart." The word *nepeš* means a "soul" or "spirit," whereas *nāpšəkā* means "your soul or spirit." *Nepeš* נֶפֶשׁ ("soul") has no corresponding word in colloquial English. This word is tied to the origins of humanity, as described in Genesis 2:7: "Then the LORD God formed man of the dust of the ground, and breathed into his nostrils the breath of life; and man became a living soul." In the Jewish tradition, the words *ûbəkol-nāpšəkā* are generally interpreted to mean that God wants his people to serve him always, even if it costs them their lives.

In Genesis 2:7, the phrase "living soul" is the translation of *nepeš ḥayyāh.* *Ḥayyāh* can either refer to a wild animal or

46

something living. The *nepeš* is what physically animates a body, and it is what motivates humans in the world of action. We can reasonably conclude from Genesis 2:7 that the soul of humans comes directly from God, who "breathed" the soul, the "breath of life," into the man he created.

Lastly, the preposition בְּ (*bə-*), translated in this passage as "with," means "by way of." The Hebrew preposition affects the reading of the biblical text. Using the words *by way of* might help us better understand that in Deuteronomy 10:12 Moses is telling the people of Israel that they must love and serve God *by way of* their souls—their very lives.

From this perspective, the phrase "with all thy heart and with all thy soul" in Deuteronomy 10:12 does not only imply the involvement of emotion or intellect. *Nepeš* symbolizes action. One possible conclusion is that seeking God does not occur only through high-minded pursuits. In this view, no exceptional talents or intelligence are required to be able to fully love God. To love God, a person needs heart and soul.

בְּכָל־לְבָבְךָ
וּבְכָל־נַפְשְׁךָ

בְּכוֹר

bəḵôr

firstborn

בְּכוֹר - bəkôr

וְאָמַרְתָּ אֶל־פַּרְעֹה כֹּה אָמַר יְהוָה בְּנִי בְכֹרִי יִשְׂרָאֵל

"And thou shalt say unto Pharaoh:
Thus saith the LORD: Israel is My son, My first-born."
Exodus 4:22

The Hebrew term *bəkôr* or *bəkôrê* has many connotations. *Bəkôr* בְּכוֹר ("firstborn") is used frequently in the Bible in the literal sense. For example, in the story of Jacob and Esau, Esau is the firstborn son of Isaac and therefore entitled to gain his father's blessing (a firstborn son received a double inheritance). However, Jacob pretends to be Esau, the firstborn, and deceives Isaac in order to steal his brother's blessing. "Jacob said to his father, 'I am Esau your firstborn. I have done as you told me; now sit up and eat of my game, that your soul may bless me' " (Genesis 27:19, ESV).

We see this in Genesis 36:15, where Eliphaz is referred to as the Esau's firstborn: "These are the chiefs of the sons of Esau: the sons of Eliphaz the first-born of Esau." Not only is a *bəḵôr* firstborn, but he has to be the first issue of every womb, man or beast. In Exodus 13:2, God tells Moses: "Sanctify unto Me all the first-born, whatsoever openeth the womb among the children of Israel, both of man and of beast, it is Mine." If a baby was stillborn, for instance, then any baby born to the same mother after that would not be considered firstborn.

In Exodus 11:5, the word is used as a collective term, even though it is in a singular form: "And all the first-born in the land of Egypt shall die, from the first-born of Pharaoh that sitteth upon his throne, even unto the first-born of the maid-servant that is behind the mill; and all the first-born of cattle." This verse tells us that every *bəḵôr* died, instead of using the plural form *bəḵôrôṭ*.

However, the word *bəḵôr* sometimes carries a different connotation than just the traditional meaning of a first-born child. *Bəḵôr* can also refer to greatness. For instance, in Exodus 4:22 God says, "Israel is My son, My first-born." Isaiah 14:30 says, "The first-born [*bəḵôrê*] of the poor shall feed, and the needy shall lie down in safety." "My first-born" and *bəḵôrê* refer to princes or great people in both verses, according to Rashi,

bəḵôr

בְּכוֹר

"firstborn"

First out of the womb
—Exodus 13:2

Heir
—Genesis 27:19

Exemplar
—Psalm 89:27–28

who makes the connection to Psalm 89:28,[6] where God says about David, "I also will appoint him first-born, the highest of the kings of the earth." Here we see that the word "first-born" does not mean the literal first child, for David is the youngest son of Jesse (1 Samuel 16:11). Instead, the word in Hebrew connotes a person who is a standard-bearer, "the highest of the kings of the earth," as if David is a role model, or the quintessential example of a king.

As we consider this Hebrew word *bəkôr* and its meanings—literal firstborn son, a person of greatness, and a role model—we can deepen our understanding of how the biblical writers viewed various human relationships with God.

בְּכוֹר

בֵּית
תְּפִלָּה

bêṯ təp̄illāh

house of prayer

bêṭ təp̄illāh - בֵּית תְּפִלָּה

וַהֲבִיאוֹתִים אֶל־הַר קָדְשִׁי וְשִׂמַּחְתִּים
בְּבֵית תְּפִלָּתִי עוֹלוֹתֵיהֶם וְזִבְחֵיהֶם
לְרָצוֹן עַל־מִזְבְּחִי כִּי בֵיתִי בֵּית־תְּפִלָּה
יִקָּרֵא לְכָל־הָעַמִּים

"Even them will I bring to My holy mountain, And make them
joyful in My house of prayer; their burnt-offerings and their
sacrifices shall be acceptable upon Mine altar; for My house
shall be called a house of prayer for all peoples."
Isaiah 56:7

Starting with God's promise to Abram, that through him "all the families of the earth shall be blessed" (Genesis 12:3, ESV), biblical writers emphasize God's desire to make himself known—not just to the people of Israel, but to every nation. This idea is expressed in Psalm 22:27: "All the ends of the earth shall remember and turn to the Lord, and all the families of the nations shall worship before you" (ESV).

This emphasis on people from every nation worshiping God also appears in less prominent aspects of the Hebrew Bible, specifically in the *bêṭ təp̄illāh* (בֵּית תְּפִלָּה). *Bêṭ təp̄illāh* literally means "a house of prayer." In

Isaiah 56:7 it refers to the temple. This verse is notable for its mix of ethnic inclusiveness and traditional customs from ancient Israel.

Looking at the entire chapter, Isaiah 56 presents us with two noticeable themes: salvation and inclusiveness. The first is found in Isaiah 56:1, in which God says, "Keep justice, and do righteousness, for soon my salvation will come, and my righteousness be revealed" (ESV).

The second theme, inclusiveness, appears primarily in Isaiah 56:3: "Let not the foreigner who has joined himself to the LORD, say, 'The LORD will surely separate me from his people'" (ESV). Then, in Isaiah 56:6–7, the inclusiveness theme develops further when God says, "And the foreigners who join themselves to the LORD, to minister to him, to love the name of the LORD, and to be his servants, everyone who keeps the Sabbath and does not profane it, and who holds fast my covenant—these I will bring to my holy mountain, and make them joyful in my house of prayer" (ESV).

Isaiah 56 can be seen as a statement about God's desire to include all people who fear God in his salvation and in his house of prayer. What we see in these verses is a God who opens access for everyone who worships him, regardless of ethnicity or nationality.

While examining the meaning of an open and inclusive house of prayer (*bêṯ tǝp̄illāh*), we might also consider new ways to open our lives and homes to those around us.

בֵּית
תְּפִלָּה

bəṣelem ʾĕlōhîm

in the image of God

bəṣelem ʾĕlōhîm - בְּצֶלֶם אֱלֹהִים

וַיִּבְרָא אֱלֹהִים אֶת־הָאָדָם בְּצַלְמוֹ
בְּצֶלֶם אֱלֹהִים בָּרָא אֹתוֹ זָכָר וּנְקֵבָה
בָּרָא אֹתָם

*"And God created man in His own image, in the image of God
created He him; male and female created He them."*
Genesis 1:27

What does it mean to be a human being? How might our views of human origins affect the way we view ourselves? These questions are addressed in a short biblical phrase that says people are created "in the image of God." In Hebrew, this phrase is *bəṣelem ʾĕlōhîm* (בְּצֶלֶם אֱלֹהִים), and it can be interpreted in many different ways. The implications of each viewpoint are significant.

The singular form for *God* is used throughout the story of creation, except for in Genesis 1:26, where a plural pronoun is used to refer to God: "Let us make man in our image, after our likeness." In the Jewish tradition, many biblical scholars interpret the plural "us" as God consulting the angels about the creation of humanity. Many in the Christian tradition hold that the plural term expresses the notion of a trinity, one God in three persons—Father, Son, and Holy Spirit—a perfect relationship.

Regardless of your viewpoint, the next two verses clarify that, according to Genesis, only one God created humanity. Genesis 1:27–28 says, "So God created man in his own image, in the image of God he created him; male and female he created them. And God blessed them. And God said to them, 'Be fruitful and multiply and fill the earth and subdue it, and have dominion over the fish of the sea and over the birds of the heavens and over every living thing that moves on the earth' " (ESV).

Many questions exist surrounding how humans are made "in the image of God." Genesis 1 gives no physical description of God, and there is no indication in the Genesis narrative that Adam and Eve have any power to create ex nihilo the way God does in the creation story. Some people explain that humans reflect God's nature. One part of his character can be seen in his desire for people to have dominion over parts of creation. He tells them to "subdue" the earth and "have dominion" over

bəṣelem ʾĕlōhîm

בְּצֶלֶם אֱלֹהִים

"in the image of God"

Having dominion over creation
—Genesis 1:26

Incredibly valuable
—Genesis 9:6

As God to Adam, Adam to Seth
—Genesis 5:3

the animals. Some people like to interpret this by saying humans are to serve as stewards of creation.

Genesis 2:15 says, "The LORD God took the man and put him in the garden of Eden to work it and keep it" (ESV). In this verse we can see that God gives humanity a certain responsibility and purpose in the world. Therefore, being made in the image of God perhaps means that humans share in God's work as active participants in the world.

The idea of being created in the image of God can inspire us to reflect and study more about the character of God and what it means to be human.

בְּצֶלֶם
אֱלֹהִים

בְּרָכָה

וּקְלָלָה

bərāḵāh ûqəlālāh

a blessing and a curse

bərāḵāh ûqəlālāh - בְּרָכָה וּקְלָלָה

רְאֵה אָנֹכִי נֹתֵן לִפְנֵיכֶם הַיּוֹם
בְּרָכָה וּקְלָלָה

"Behold, I set before you this day a blessing and a curse."
Deuteronomy 11:26

T here are many decisions in life that are complex and full of uncertainty. But in the book of Deuteronomy, we find what appears to be a straightforward choice.

In Deuteronomy 10:1–2, God calls Moses up the mountain to receive the Ten Commandments for the second time. After receiving the commandments, Moses tells the Israelites that these laws of God will enable them to flourish if they are followed (Deuteronomy 11:8–15). Moses appears to be impressing on the Israelites the crucial importance of the commandments, including for future generations (Deuteronomy 11:19).

In that context, we come across the Hebrew phrase *bərāḵāh ûqəlālāh* (בְּרָכָה וּקְלָלָה), which is usually translated

61

as "a blessing and a curse." Deuteronomy 11:26–28 says, "See, I am setting before you today a blessing and a curse: the blessing, if you obey the commandments of the LORD your God, which I command you today, and the curse, if you do not obey the commandments of the

bərākāh ûqəlālāh

בְּרָכָה וּקְלָלָה

"a blessing and a curse"

A way to gain God's blessing and a way to incur God's curse
—Deuteronomy 11:26–28

Choosing Israel or choosing Canaan
—Deuteronomy 11:29–32

LORD your God, but turn aside from the way that I am commanding you today, to go after other gods that you have not known" (ESV).

The straightforward choice in these verses—between receiving "a blessing and a curse"—appears in the initial phrase (verse 26), and the details appear in the latter part of the passage. The inclusion of the word *and*—Hebrew *vav* (ו)—in the phrase can cause some people to view this as if God is offering the Israelites a blessing and a curse simultaneously. Some Hebrew scholars, however, will explain that both are being offered—but people can take either one *or* the other.

God presents to the people of Israel a simple reality in this passage from Deuteronomy, and the outcomes of their lives hinge on how they respond. We see two options: they can abide by God's law and flourish, or they can choose not to abide by God's law and face increased hardship.

From these words, it is evident that obedience brings God's blessing and rebellion brings God's curse.

According to Deuteronomy, God's laws help his people to make wise decisions as they journey through life. This principle is expressed by the psalmist who wrote Psalm 119: "Your word is a lamp to my feet and a light to my path" (verse 105, ESV). It's possible to conclude from these words that God has given his people what they need to make good and wise choices.

Perhaps the clarity and simplicity of God's command to the people of Israel—to choose between a blessing and a curse—can help direct us on our own paths in life.

בְּרָכָה
וּקְלָלָה

בְּרִית

bərît

covenant

בְּרִית - bərît

וַיֵּרָא יְהֹוָה אֶל־אַבְרָם וַיֹּאמֶר אֵלָיו
אֲנִי־אֵל שַׁדַּי הִתְהַלֵּךְ לְפָנַי וֶהְיֵה
תָמִים וְאֶתְּנָה בְרִיתִי בֵּינִי וּבֵינֶךָ
וְאַרְבֶּה אוֹתְךָ בִּמְאֹד מְאֹד

*"And when Abram was ninety years old and nine,
the LORD appeared to Abram, and said unto him: 'I am
God Almighty; walk before Me, and be thou wholehearted.
And I will make My covenant between Me and thee,
and will multiply thee exceedingly.' "*
Genesis 17:1–2

A t almost every wedding, the bride and groom sign a legal
document provided by the state that authenticates their
new marital status. As a legal document, it serves an important
function, but few would say that the license expresses the heart

and soul of the marriage. The true commitment in a marriage is expressed by the ceremony, the vows, and the rings.

To better understand what the Bible says about the relational commitment between God and people, it can be helpful to study an important Hebrew word that distinguishes between a contractual relationship and an alliance.

The Hebrew word *bərît* בְּרִית ("covenant") is frequently used in the first five books of the Bible and in the prophetic books as well. It appears in Genesis 9:8–13, in which God establishes a covenant with Noah and his sons to never again destroy the earth by flood. Another example is found in Exodus 19:5, in which Moses ascends Mount Sinai and God tells him of a future covenant he wants the Israelites to honor.

In both of these examples, the term *covenant* is used to indicate a type of agreement between God and people. However, the Hebrew word *bərît* has other uses that further reveal its meaning. In several cases throughout the Bible, the Hebrew term *bərît* refers to an alliance.

We see mentions of positive alliances between Abram (later Abraham) and the Amorites in Genesis 14:13; between Abraham and the Abimelech in Genesis 21:27–32; and between Solomon and Hiram, king of Tyre, in 1 Kings 5:1–12.

bərît

בְּרִית

"covenant"

Covenant
—Genesis 17:1–2

Circumcision
—Genesis 17:11

Alliance
—1 Kings 5:2–6

On the other hand, in Exodus 23:32, the Israelites are told to avoid alliances with the nations within the land of Canaan. Additionally, in Isaiah 33:8 we see that an enemy of Israel is said to have "broken [their] covenant" (*bərît* בְּרִית) with Israel. Moreover, what is usually translated as "all your allies" (ESV) in Obadiah 7 would literally be translated as "all the men of your alliance" (כֹּל אַנְשֵׁי בְרִיתֶךָ *kōl ʾanšē bərîtekā*).

Through these biblical portraits, and by understanding the nuances of the Hebrew word *bərît*, it is possible to see that God doesn't seem interested in making legally binding contracts with people; rather, God forms alliances with them. We can perhaps conclude that God desires heartfelt relationships with his people that are based on mutual commitment.

בְּרִית

חַג

ḥaḡ

festival

ḥag - חַג

שָׁלֹשׁ פְּעָמִים בַּשָּׁנָה יֵרָאֶה כָּל זְכוּרְךָ
אֶל פְּנֵי הָאָדֹן יְהֹוָה

*"Three times in the year all thy males shall appear before the
Lord GOD."*
Exodus 23:17

T he Hebrew term *ḥag* (חַג) refers to three pilgrimage
festivals: Pesach, or Passover (Leviticus 23:5–21);
Sukkot, or Tabernacles (Leviticus 23:33–43); and
Shavuot, or Pentecost, the harvest festival (Exodus 34:22).
The Israelites would make the trip to Jerusalem for the
occasion and then make sacrifices at the temple. This
was done to honor God and to reinforce the people's
connection with him.

In English, *ḥag* is usually translated as "festival,"
which is a partially correct meaning. The English fails
to display the unique importance of a pilgrimage holiday, which is conveyed in the Hebrew *ḥag*. A more

thorough under-
standing of the He-
brew word, as it is
used in other books
of the Bible, can be
helpful for extract-
ing the richness of
the word's meaning.

For example,
Amos 5 exempli-
fies the difficulty of
translating *ḥaḡ* from
Hebrew into Eng-

ḥaḡ

חַג

"festival"

Festival/Feast for God
—Exodus 32:5

Pilgrimage festival
—Exodus 23:14–17

Sacrifice for a festival
—Amos 5:21

lish. Amos 5:21 begins, "I hate, I despise your feasts."
According to many Hebrew scholars, *ḥaḡ* ("feasts") here
refers to festive sacrifices that were offered to God. God
despised the sacrifices because the people were offering them while behaving improperly—and, therefore,
hypocritically—before God. The word *ḥaḡ* in this verse
is alternately translated as "feast days" in the King
James Version and "religious festivals" in the New In-
ternational Version. These are accurate translations in a
technical sense, but they don't convey the importance
of a *ḥaḡ* relative to other biblical holidays.

As previously stated, *ḥaḡ* refers to pilgrimage festivals, when the people would travel to Jerusalem
specifically in order to offer sacrifices to God at the
temple, in obedience to God's commandment in Exodus 23:17. In this way, the word *ḥaḡ* conveys the rich
meaning and power of people obediently following

God's commandment and celebrating their commitment to him.

חַג

ḥēṭ(')

sin: to miss the target

ḥēṭ(') - חֵטְא

וְאִם־נֶפֶשׁ אַחַת תֶּחֱטָא בִשְׁגָגָה מֵעַם
הָאָרֶץ בַּעֲשֹׂתָהּ אַחַת מִמִּצְוֹת יְהוָה
אֲשֶׁר לֹא־תֵעָשֶׂינָה וְאָשֵׁם

"And if any one of the common people sin through error, in doing any of the things which the LORD hath commanded not to be done, and be guilty."
Leviticus 4:27

Most parents can tell funny stories about toddlers who innocently did something wrong without knowing it was wrong. Because small children often have no clue about the nuances of right and wrong, parents are typically merciful and seek to teach their children to avoid repeating the same errors.

The Hebrew language in Leviticus 4:27 shows us that God treats people with mercy in his response to sins committed by those who don't know God's laws. The Hebrew word for this type of sin, according to the Talmud (*Yoma* 36b), is *ḥēṭ(')* (חֵטְא).

In this verse, the word refers to *unintentional* sins committed through ignorance of the law—not through planned malice.

This definition of *ḥēṭ(')* distinguishes it from other Hebrew words for *sin*, such as "iniquity" (*'āwōn* עָוֹן) or "trespass" (*peša'* פֶּשַׁע), which describe sins committed with varying degrees of evil intent.

In addition to denoting unintentional sins, *ḥēṭ(')* can sometimes denote sin in general. For example, the confession recited on the Day of Atonement, which is a litany of personal sins arranged in acrostic order, begins each line with the Hebrew phrase על חטא שחטאנו לפניך ("For the sin we have committed against you").

As we look more closely at what the Bible reveals about the nature of sin, the book of Judges gives us interesting perspectives. Judges 20 describes the battle of the tribe of Benjamin with the rest of the nation of Israel. The verse describes an elite force of 700 young Benjaminite warriors, each of whom "could sling a stone at a hair and not miss" (Judges 20:16, ESV). The phrase used in the Bible for "and not miss" is *wəlō(') yaḥăṭi'* (וְלֹא יַחֲטִא). The word *yachti* derives from the same root as the word *ḥēṭ(')*.

What does the incredible shooting accuracy of snipers have to

ḥēṭ(')

חֵטְא

"sin: to miss the target"

Sin (in general)
—Genesis 41:9;
Deuteronomy 9:18

Unintentional sin
—Leviticus 4:27

Guilt related to an act of sin
—Numbers 27:3

Punishment for sin
—Leviticus 20:20

do with our understanding of the transgression of God's laws? It is possible to infer from the verse in Judges that the meaning of the word *ḥēṭ(')* is "to miss a target." From this perspective, the image of a sniper shooting at a target and missing can be seen as a metaphor for sin. The target is God's law, a perfect reference point, and sin is a failure to hit that target.

In Genesis 2:16–17 God instructs Adam to eat from any tree except the tree of the knowledge of good and evil. God tells him that if he chooses to reject his instruction about the tree, he will "surely die." There is no indication in these verses that God is attempting to control Adam's choice. He appears to be giving Adam a free choice between good and evil. If Adam and Eve "hit the target" by obeying God, they will live. If they "miss the target," they will fall into hardships. (These hardships are described in Genesis 3:16–19.)

In many stories in the Bible, God is portrayed as merciful when people miss the mark. For example, in the book of Jonah, we read about the city of Nineveh, where evil and violence has become prominent (Jonah 1:2, 3:8). God sends Jonah to tell the people of Nineveh to turn away from sin (Jonah 1:2). In response to Jonah's message, the king of Nineveh and its people humble themselves and turn away from violence (Jonah 3:9). As a result, God relents and does not impose punishment on them, showing his mercy and forgiveness.

The examples from the Bible where God shows mercy perhaps can be seen as God giving people a chance to adjust the next arrow's trajectory when they miss their target so they do not repeat the same mistakes.

חֲטָא

ḥeseḏ

loving-kindness

ḥesed - חֶסֶד

הִגִּיד לְךָ אָדָם מַה־טּוֹב וּמָה־יְהוָה דּוֹרֵשׁ
מִמְּךָ כִּי אִם־עֲשׂוֹת מִשְׁפָּט וְאַהֲבַת חֶסֶד
וְהַצְנֵעַ לֶכֶת עִם אֱלֹהֶיךָ

"It hath been told thee, O man, what is good, and what the
LORD doth require of thee: Only to do justly, and to love mercy,
and to walk humbly with thy God."

Micah 6:8

In Micah 6:6–7, the prophet asks if God is pleased with burnt-offerings, calves, oil, or even child sacrifice as a means of setting things right with God. Then Micah provides a simple but profound answer. He says that God wants his people to "do justly, and to love mercy, and to walk humbly with [their] God" (Micah 6:8).

Ḥesed (חֶסֶד) is the Hebrew word Micah uses for "love mercy" (also translated as "love kindness"). *Ḥesed* is related to the word *ḥāsîd* (חָסִיד), which conveys a deep-felt kindness and concern for the needs of others. Ḥeseḏ refers to kindness in Genesis 21:23, where Abimelech reminds Abraham of all his kindness to him: "Now therefore swear to me here by God that you will not deal falsely with me or with my descendants or with my posterity,

ḥeseḏ

חֶסֶד

"loving-kindness"

Showing mercy
—Micah 6:8

Mutual kindness
—Genesis 21:23

A shameful or disgraceful thing
—Leviticus 20:17

but as I have dealt kindly with you, so you will deal with me and with the land where you have sojourned" (ESV).

Moreover, ḥāsîḏ expresses what it means to be pious ("devoted" or "devout"). This word shows us that, in Hebrew, kindness and piety are inextricably linked. This strong connection between kindness and piety is exemplified in two Jewish groups who called themselves ḥāsîḏîm, the plural of ḥāsîḏ. The earlier was an Ashkenazi Jewish group in the twelfth and thirteenth centuries that played an important role in the life of European Jews. The later movement of ḥāsîḏîm started with the Baal Shem Tov in the eighteenth century. Both groups are well known for supporting kindness and piety in daily life.

Interestingly, the term ḥeseḏ can also mean the opposite of the examples cited above. We see a derogatory usage of the word ḥeseḏ in Proverbs 25:10, where the verse tells us, "Lest he that heareth it revile thee." Ḥeseḏ here refers to revulsion or shame. Rabbi Ibn Ezra explains that *ḥesed* is used in Leviticus when referring to cases of extraordinary illicit sexual relations.[7] Leviticus 20:17, for example, describes acts of incest as *ḥesed*—"a shameful thing" or "a disgrace" (ESV). People tend to revile those who engage in these types of forbidden behaviors.

חֶסֶד

חָכְמָה

ḥoḵmāh

wisdom

ḥokmāh - חָכְמָה

יִרְאַת יְהוָה רֵאשִׁית דָּעַת חָכְמָה
וּמוּסָר אֱוִילִים בָּזוּ

"The fear of the LORD is the beginning of knowledge; but the foolish despise wisdom and discipline."

Proverbs 1:7

W hen we enter discussions about the origins of the universe, we usually focus on the fascinating issues related to physics, cosmology, and astronomy. But when was the last time you heard of wisdom being included in the role of creation?

In the book of Proverbs, the Hebrew word *ḥokmāh* חָכְמָה ("wisdom") points to an often overlooked factor that the Bible describes as being foundational in creation. Referring to wisdom, Proverbs 8:22–23 says, "The LORD possessed me at the beginning of his work, the first of his acts of old. Ages ago I was set up, at the first, before the beginning of the earth" (ESV).

This theme continues through verse 30, with each verse pointing to an element of creation that is designed by God with *ḥokmāh*. In what ways can we understand the role of wisdom in the biblical account of God's creation? A robust understanding can be gained by studying several other similar Hebrew concepts.

Three Hebrew concepts fit the English notion of wisdom: *ḥokmāh*, *daʿaṯ*, and *bînāh*. The first is primarily what we saw in Proverbs, but the meaning of *ḥokmāh* is more related to knowing the axiom from which all subsequent things ensue. *Daʿaṯ* is basically unified knowledge that inclusively encompasses all that a person knows. Lastly, *bînāh* is best understood as a deep intuition, which is a contributing factor to knowledge.

Understanding *ḥokmāh* in light of these other Hebrew words related to wisdom, we can hone our understanding of its use in Proverbs as playing a role in creation. *Ḥokmāh* is all-encompassing, as it is intrinsically linked to the foundations of creation and refers to a knowledge of the substratum of creation from which all things derive. From this basis, we can see why *ḥokmāh* is the attribute of God related to creation in this section of Proverbs.

Many people spend extensive time and

ḥokmāh

חָכְמָה

"wisdom"

Wisdom personified as speech
—Proverbs 1:20

*Wisdom as foundational
in creation*
—Proverbs 8:22–23

energy pursuing knowledge about their professions, politics, financial markets, and many other aspects of daily life. These are often healthy pursuits, of course, but knowledge is not the same as wisdom. Therefore, it's possible that developing our understanding of the wisdom that is *ḥokmāh* can bring many benefits to our lives.

As Proverbs 1:7 famously says, "The fear of the LORD is the beginning of knowledge [*da'at*]; But the foolish despise wisdom [*ḥokmāh*] and discipline." This verse implies that God is the quintessential exemplar and source of knowledge and wisdom. To some Bible readers, this could indicate that having a relationship with God leads to living a wise life.

Much of the book of Proverbs is dedicated to specific applications of wisdom in every area of life. As you consider the term *ḥokmāh* and the book of Proverbs, perhaps you might ask what steps you can take to grow in wisdom.

חָכְמָה

gēr

foreigner

גֵּר - gēr

וְגֵר לֹא תִלְחָץ וְאַתֶּם יְדַעְתֶּם אֶת־נֶפֶשׁ
הַגֵּר כִּי גֵרִים הֱיִיתֶם בְּאֶרֶץ מִצְרָיִם

"And a stranger shalt thou not oppress; for ye know the heart of a
stranger, seeing ye were strangers in the land of Egypt."
Exodus 23:9

The Bible contains many stories about displaced people. From Abraham in Canaan, to Moses in the Sinai desert, to the Israelites in Egypt, Assyria, and Babylon—the Bible's emphasis on this theme is difficult to miss.

The Hebrew word *gēr* ("foreigner") comes from the root גּוּר, which means to "sojourn" or "dwell," and is commonly translated as "stranger." The word, common in the first five books of the Bible, is often used for people living in a nation other than their own. For example, the term *gēr* (plural *gērîm*) is used in a prophecy given to Abraham about the Israelites (Genesis 15:13) and to describe Abraham living in Hebron (Genesis 23:4).

Being a *gēr* ("foreigner") was common in the ancient world as people moved for cultural or economic reasons to another region and lived as noncitizens. In ancient Athens, a foreigner living in the city received some of the privileges of being a Greek citizen. This parallels the biblical idea of a "stranger."

gēr

גֵּר

"foreigner"

Stranger/Foreigner
—Genesis 15:13

Non-citizen resident
—Leviticus 25:47

A convert to Judaism
—Modern Hebrew usage

Jewish tradition differentiates various types of foreigners who lived among the people of Israel. A *gēr tôšaḇ*, described in Leviticus 25:47, was a foreigner who accepted some of the commandments given to the Israelites. This person committed not to serve idols but continued to eat nonkosher animals. A *gēr ṣedeq*, on the other hand, accepted all the commandments and was considered a true follower of the God of Israel. Interestingly, the Modern Hebrew *gēr* has been transformed from "stranger" into the term used to describe a convert to Judaism.

When it comes to hosting a foreigner in one's homeland, Leviticus 19:33 and Deuteronomy 24:14 speak about being hospitable without oppressing the stranger. Regulations were also given for the *gērîm* and the Israelites within Israel. For example, Deuteronomy 14:21 distinguishes between a *gēr* and an Israelite: a *gēr* can eat from a carcass while an

Israelite cannot. Yet, Exodus 20:10 says that the *gērîm* must observe the Sabbath like the Israelite. Here we see a difference in the expectations of a *gēr tôšab* and a *gēr ṣedeq*, as described earlier.

The biblical passages that provide God's expecations of the Israelites in their treatment of foreigners promote an overarching goal that can apply to us today: to bring harmony between the communities of foreigners and native-born citizens, and to treat every individual with dignity.

This is emphasized in Leviticus 19:34, where we find a command to treat all foreigners with love: "You shall treat the stranger [*gēr*] who sojourns with you as the native among you, and you shall love him as yourself, for you were strangers [*gērîm*] in the land of Egypt: I am the LORD your God" (ESV).

The meaning of the Hebrew word *gēr* in the Bible, and the biblical commands related to humane treatment of strangers and foreigners—including refugees—can help us consider how we should approach the millions of people worldwide who find themselves in similar situations today.

גֵּר

גֹּאֵל

gōʾēl

to avenge

gō'ēl - גֹּאֵל

פִּצְחוּ רַנְּנוּ יַחְדָּו חָרְבוֹת יְרוּשָׁלָָ
כִּי־נִחַם יְהוָה עַמּוֹ גָּאַל יְרוּשָׁלָָ

"Break forth into joy, sing together,
Ye waste places of Jerusalem;
For the LORD hath comforted His people,
He hath redeemed Jerusalem."
Isaiah 52:9

The Bible provides many rich insights about principles of justice, but one that is often overlooked is found in the Hebrew word *gō'ēl* (גֹּאֵל). The word is not cleanly translated into English, but two common translations of *gō'ēl* are "to avenge" and "to redeem."

A rudimentary understanding of *gō'ēl* can be gained from looking at Numbers 35. This passage addresses the differences between murder and manslaughter, and how these differences relate to Levite cities of refuge. With that in mind, Numbers 35:19 refers to an "avenger of blood" (gō'ēl גָּאַל), a kinsman of a murder victim who has the right under very specific circumstances to kill the victim's murderer. This might sound like straightforward vengeance in English, but other passages can provide us with a clearer understanding of *gō'ēl*.

The background of the "avenger of blood" meaning of *gō'ēl* is found in a familiar biblical story: Cain and Abel. After Cain kills his brother, God says, "What have you done? The voice of your brother's blood is crying to me from the ground" (Genesis 4:10, ESV).

This metaphor of "blood crying" provides us with some additional context for understanding *gō'ēl*. While an "avenger of blood" might sound like vengeance rather than redemption to the modern ear, it means here to rectify a grievous evil that led to the loss of a life. It's possible to see from these Hebrew meanings that restoring what has been destroyed is central to redemption.

Isaiah 52:9 says, "Break forth together into singing, you waste places of Jerusalem, for the LORD has comforted his people; he has redeemed Jerusalem" (ESV). In this verse, "redeemed" is the same *gō'ēl* that is used to mean "avenge." This serves to reinforce the notion that vengeance in the Bible functions to rectify

gō'ēl

גָּאַל

"to avenge"

Avenge
—Numbers 35:19

Redeem
—Isaiah 52:9

Perform loving mercy
—Psalm 103:4

wrongs. For this reason, Isaiah 52:9 expresses so much joy about the redemption of God.

This is approaching the full sense of the word *gōʾēl*, but David provides additional insights in Psalm 103:4. David writes that it is God "who redeems [*gōʾēl*] your life from the pit, who crowns you with steadfast love and mercy" (ESV). *Gōʾēl* from God, as we see in this verse, has none of the troubling aspects of human vengeance. According to Psalm 103:4, God's redemption is rooted in "love and mercy."

These traits can be seen when considering how God responds to Cain after killing his brother. God requires justice, but God does not kill Cain; instead, he curses him to live in exile as a nomad. God's response can be seen as justice combined with mercy.

גָּאַל

גּוֹלָה

gôlāh

exile

gôlāh - גּוֹלָה

כִּי לֹא יַעֲשֶׂה אֲדֹנָי יְהוִה דָּבָר כִּי
אִם־גָּלָה סוֹדוֹ אֶל־עֲבָדָיו הַנְּבִיאִים

*"For the Lord GOD will do nothing, But He revealeth His
counsel unto His servants the prophets."*

Amos 3:7

Throughout the Hebrew Bible, stories are told that provide a history of the Israelites and the numerous exiles they endure over generations.

The Hebrew words *gôlāh* גּוֹלָה ("exile," as a verb) and *gālûṭ* גָּלוּת ("exile," as a noun) describe the displacement that happens to the Israelites throughout their biblical history. Both of these words share a root, *gālāh* (גָּלָה), that means "to reveal" or "to exile." An *exile* is fundamentally used to describe a people being removed from a homeland, so this makes perfect sense on a basic level. Moreover, *gālāh* also refers to "revealing," in the sense conveyed in Amos 3:7, which says, "For the Lord GOD does nothing without revealing his secret to his servants the prophets" (ESV).

In the Bible, the use of *gôlāh* and *gālût* are generally reserved for the Babylonian exile, but they also apply to other major displacements in Jewish history. These include Abram and his family moving to Canaan (Genesis 12:1–9); Jacob's children moving

gôlāh

גּוֹלָה

"exile"

Captives
—2 Kings 24:14

The exiles
—Zechariah 6:10

Reveal
—Amos 3:7

to Egypt (Genesis 45–46); the Israelites' escape from slavery in Egypt after 430 years in captivity (Exodus 12–14); and the people of Judah being taken as captives to Babylon (2 Kings 24). In these examples, it is possible to see a pattern emerge.

In the first example above, Abram (later Abraham) is commanded by God to go to the land of Canaan. God says to Abram in Genesis 12:1, "Go from your country and your kindred and your father's house to the land that I will show you" (ESV). Upon Abram's arrival in Canaan, God gives him a new promise: "To your offspring I will give this land" (Genesis 12:7, ESV). Abram is not displaced in vain; he is given the land for his descendants.

A similar grant is given after the Israelites escape captivity in Egypt and are wandering in the desert. In Exodus 33:1, God says to Moses, "Depart; go up from here, you and the people whom you have brought up out of the land of Egypt, to the land of which I swore to Abraham, Isaac, and

Jacob, saying, 'To your offspring I will give it' " (ESV). The Israelites eventually regain their land, but during the desert years of exile they also receive the Torah, which is revealed at Mount Sinai (Exodus 19–20, 34). The people benefit from the hardship.

The exile in Babylon advances this idea further. At the end of the Babylonian captivity, King Cyrus grants the Jews the freedom to return to their homeland of Judah (2 Chronicles 36:22–23). Yet, Babylon is where the Talmud is compiled by the Jewish community that remained by choice in the land of exile.

As we reflect on these biblical accounts of exile, it is possible to see, as the Israelites discovered, that good often presents itself even in the midst of difficult circumstances.

גּוֹלָה

hebel

vanity

hebel - הֶבֶל

וַיֵּלְכוּ אַחֲרֵי הַהֶבֶל וַיֶּהְבָּלוּ

"And they went after things of nought, and became nought."
2 Kings 17:15

The word *idolatry* can conjure up images of statues carved or sculpted by artisans and sold by merchants for profit. But there are many different types of idols presented in the Bible.

For example, in Jeremiah 22:17, God says that the people have set their hearts on the idol of material wealth, which leads them to "dishonest gain . . . oppression and violence" (ESV). And in Ezekiel 28:1, God speaks against the ruler of Tyre, who sets himself up as an idol: "Because thy heart is lifted up, and thou hast said: I am a god, I sit in the seat of God, in the heart of the seas; yet thou art man, and not God, though thou didst set thy heart as the heart of God."

These biblical examples, among many others, might lead us to conclude that idolatry is much more widespread and alluring than we imagine.

Regardless of the type of idol, the Bible often states that idolatry is futile. The English term *worthless* translates as *hebel* (הֶבֶל) in Hebrew. In Modern Hebrew, it means "vapor." It is used figuratively to mean "vanity" in the sense of worthlessness or futility. A perfect expression of *hebel* is found in Ecclesiastes 1:2–3, which says: "Vanity [*hebel*] of vanities, says the Preacher, vanity of vanities! All is vanity. What does a man gain by all the toil at which he toils under the sun?" (ESV). These verses show how *hebel* is used for worthless efforts and inherent futility.

The prophet Jeremiah also expresses the worthlessness of idolatry. He writes: "Every man is stupid and without knowledge; every goldsmith is put to shame by his idols, for his images are false, and there is no breath in them. They are worthless, a work of delusion; at the time of their punishment they shall perish" (Jeremiah 10:14–15, ESV).

The futility of idolatry is also evident in the use of the word *hebel* (הֶבֶל) in 2 Kings 17. In verses 13–14, the people of Israel and Judah are warned to repent and follow God's commandments, but they continue to spurn God to follow worthless idols. "They despised his statutes and his covenant that he made with their fathers and

hebel

הֶבֶל

"vanity"

Vanity
—Ecclesiastes 1:2–3

Worthless/Futile
—2 Kings 17:15

Empty
—Jeremiah 10:14

Vapor
—Modern Hebrew usage

the warnings that he gave them. They went after false idols and became false, and they followed the nations that were around them, concerning whom the LORD had commanded them that they should not do like them" (2 Kings 17:15, ESV).

Looking more closely at 2 Kings 17:15, the words "became false" (or "became nought," as they appear in the JPS Tanakh 1917) form the denominative form of *hebel* and function like a verb. In Hebrew, this means that worshiping an idol does not only make the worshiper like the idol; it makes the worshiper a manifestation of the idol's hollowness and emptiness. The worshiper believes that the idol will bestow certain powers, but idolatry just reveals the worshiper's delusion—often in calamity. As Psalm 7:15 says: "He makes a pit, digging it out, and falls into the hole that he has made" (ESV).

Understanding the underlying relationship between idolatry and *hebel*—vanity—can assist us in an assessment of today's culture and the modern idols that might be present.

הֶבֶל

קָדוֹשׁ

qāḏôš

holy

קָדוֹשׁ - qādôš

דַּבֵּר אֶל־כָּל־עֲדַת בְּנֵי־יִשְׂרָאֵל וְאָמַרְתָּ
אֲלֵהֶם קְדֹשִׁים תִּהְיוּ כִּי קָדוֹשׁ אֲנִי יְהוָה
אֱלֹהֵיכֶם

*"Speak unto all the congregation of the children of Israel, and say
unto them: Ye shall be holy; for I the LORD your God am holy."*
Leviticus 19:2

Why is it that one person sees meaning and dignity in their work whereas another sees their work as something degrading? Perhaps part of the answer can be found in God's call in Leviticus 19 for the people of Israel to "be holy." A deeper reflection on what *holy* means in Hebrew can help us change the way we interpret even the most mundane aspects of life.

What does it mean to be holy? Some people imagine that being holy is related to living an isolated life on a faraway mountaintop. However, this view is quite different from biblical commands to be engaged in the world. For example, in Genesis 1:28, God commands Adam and Eve to "be fruitful, and multiply, and replenish the earth." In addition, Genesis 2:15 states, "The Lord GOD took the man and put him in the garden of Eden to work it and keep it"

qāḏôš

קָדוֹשׁ

"holy"

Holy
—Amos 2:7

Sanctified
—Numbers 17:2

The temple in Jerusalem
—2 Chronicles 29:7

(ESV). And the prophet Jeremiah called the Jewish exiles to build houses, plant gardens, raise children, and to "seek the peace of the city" (Jeremiah 29:5–7). From these verses, we might conclude that God expects his people to be engaged in making the world a better place.

However, the Hebrew word for holy is *qāḏôš* (קודש), which literally means "set aside" and "dedicated for a sacred purpose." Moreover, *qāḏôš* can mean "consecrated." In this way, the idea of being dedicated to something or someone is connected to the nature of the Hebrew meaning of *holiness*.

From this perspective of holiness, a person's intent and motivation are related to the holiness of everything they do. For example, when we consume a meal not merely to fill the belly but to provide sustenance for the body so that it can do God's work, then eating can become an act of holiness dedicated to God. Accordingly, everything we do and all our possessions can be used to participate in God's purposes—and are thereby holy, or set apart for God.

Understanding this concept of holiness perhaps gives us greater insight into Leviticus 19:2. Although we might believe that our work is ordinary or unimportant, we can begin to see that our work can be a way of serving God. In the course of daily life, we do our best by conducting business with integrity, and we can treat others with respect.

By understanding the Hebrew word for *holiness*, we might find inspiration to perceive our everyday routines—including our work—in a new way. We can consider ways to live holy lives every day.

קָדוֹשׁ

kippēr

atone

kippēr - כִּפֵּר

וְהָיְתָה־זֹּאת לָכֶם לְחֻקַּת עוֹלָם
לְכַפֵּר עַל בְּנֵי יִשְׂרָאֵל מִכָּל חַטֹּאתָם
אַחַת בַּשָּׁנָה

" 'And this shall be an everlasting statute unto you,
to make atonement for the children of Israel because of
all their sins once in the year.' And he did as the LORD
commanded Moses."

Leviticus 16:34

Many people struggle with feelings of guilt after behaving in ways that harm others or themselves. What do we do with the guilt that results from wrongdoing? And what form of recompense is required to right the wrongs that have been committed?

One of the ways that Jewish people address these profound questions is through Yom Kippur, or Yom HaKippurim, the Jewish Day of Atonement. Understanding the

Hebrew root for the word *atonement—kippēr*—can help us reflect on the nature of atonement in the Bible and how that might apply to questions about guilt and remorse.

We find a short description of Yom HaKippurim in Leviticus 23:27–28. God says, "Howbeit on the tenth day of this seventh month is the day of atonement; there shall be a holy convocation unto you, and ye shall afflict your souls; and ye shall bring an offering made by fire unto the LORD. And ye shall do no manner of work in that same day; for it is a day of atonement, to make atonement for you before the LORD your God." The original Hebrew in these verses uses the term אִשֶּׁה (*'iššeh*) (derived from אֵשׁ (*'ēš*), meaning "fire") to describe the offering that was required by God.

In the Jewish tradition, the phrase "ye shall afflict your souls" implies a period of fasting. Therefore, it is a somber day. But the English-only description of this day doesn't shed light on how a person's wrongdoing is being rectified. We see sorrow and lament, but no indication of recompense for those who have suffered loss as a result of sin.

The absence of any mention of recompense in these verses might indicate that atonement (*kippurîm*) is not about the legalities of wrongdoing and compensation. Instead, *kipper* is perhaps about God seeking to perfect

kippēr

כִּפֵּר

"atone"

Atone
—Leviticus 16:23–33

Appease
—Genesis 32:20–21

Ransom
—Isaiah 43:3

us, to help us be whole and free, and to restore our hearts and souls.

This viewpoint is apparent in Psalm 51:18–19. In this confessional psalm by David after he committed adultery with Bathsheba, he says, "For Thou delightest not in sacrifice, else would I give it; Thou hast no pleasure in burnt-offering. The sacrifices of God are a broken spirit; a broken and a contrite heart, O God, Thou wilt not despise."

Based on this verse, atonement (*kippurîm*) with God is not about making sacrifices; it's about having "a broken and a contrite heart." Whereas penance and sacrifices are external, the word *kipper* helps us to consider what is happening below the surface, at the level of our hearts. For David, as he says in Psalm 51, and in Leviticus 16, atonement is ultimately about standing brokenhearted before God.

כִּפֶּר

כָּבוֹד

kāḇôḏ

glory

כָּבוֹד - kābôd

מְלֹא כָל־הָאָרֶץ כְּבוֹדוֹ

"The whole earth is full of [God's] glory."
Isaiah 6:3

I magine camping in the mountains on a clear night with no moon. Countless stars fill the sky from horizon to horizon. The beauty is so overwhelming that you are not only filled with joy but also burdened with your apparent insignificance.

David writes about a similar experience that perhaps occurred while he was tending sheep through the night. "When I behold Thy heavens, the work of Thy fingers, the moon and the stars, which Thou hast established; what is man, that Thou art mindful of him? And the son of man, that Thou thinkest of him?" (Psalm 8:4–5). Based on these verses, David responds to the majesty of God's creation with both humility and awe.

The prophet Isaiah's experience with God also leaves him awestruck. In Isaiah 6, we read that Isaiah is given a vision of God sitting on a throne. The seraphim proclaim his holiness:

"Holy, holy, holy is the Lord of hosts; the whole earth is full of His glory" (verse 3). This experience with God's holiness overwhelms Isaiah. So heavy is his encounter with God that he can only say, "Woe is me! for I am undone" (verse 5).

It's possible to see a common thread in

kāḇôḏ

כָּבוֹד

"glory"

Weight of God's glory
—Exodus 20:18

Heavy
—Exodus 18:18

God's presence
—Isaiah 6:3

these cases—David under the stars and Isaiah before the seraphim. God reveals his majesty and holiness, and both men experience inspiring awe and weighty humility. Some Bible scholars would describe this type of response to God as a fear of God. Deuteronomy 10:12 says, "And now, Israel, what doth the Lord thy God require of thee, but to fear the Lord thy God, to walk in all His ways, and to love Him, and to serve the Lord thy God with all thy heart and with all thy soul."

The Hebrew word *kāḇôḏ* כָּבוֹד ("glory") can help us understand what fearing God implies. Appearing frequently in the Bible, *kavod* generally means "honor and respect," as in the case of the fifth commandment: "Honor thy father and thy mother" (Exodus 20:12).

The root of the word is derived from *kāḇēḏ* (כָּבֵד), meaning "heavy," and is used in Exodus 18:18: "You and the people with you will certainly wear yourselves out, for the thing is too heavy [כבד] for you. You are not able to do it alone"

(ESV). In this example, *kaved* invokes the idea of heaviness or weight.

Consider the inspiration and the weight a little-league baseball player feels when he gets an autograph, face-to-face, from a famous professional player. The "glory" (athletic respect and talent) of the professional player generates awe and admiration in the heart of the child. But the player's greatness also creates a heavy awareness in the young player that he might never reach such greatness. The encounter is both inspiring and weighty.

Reflecting on the *weight* of glory, Exodus 20:18 describes Moses ascending the mountain to receive the Ten Commandments. God's glory was all-encompassing, appearing to Moses as "thick darkness." The Israelites at the bottom of the mountain experienced the *heaviness* of God's glory: "When the people saw it, they trembled, and stood afar off" (Exodus 20:15). In that moment, it became obvious to everyone that God was present among them, and they were overwhelmed.

Perhaps this discussion of God's glory, and the Hebrew word *kābôḏ*, might help us consider our responses to a majestic starry night.

כָּבוֹד

kōhēn

priest

kōhēn - כֹּהֵן

לֹא־יִהְיֶה לַכֹּהֲנִים הַלְוִיִּם כָּל־שֵׁבֶט
לֵוִי חֵלֶק וְנַחֲלָה עִם־יִשְׂרָאֵל אִשֵּׁי
יְהֹוָה וְנַחֲלָתוֹ יֹאכֵלוּן

*"The priests the Levites, even all the tribe of Levi, shall have
no portion nor inheritance with Israel; they shall eat the
offerings of the LORD made by fire, and His inheritance."*
Deuteronomy 18:1

From the beginning of Israelite history, priests and Levites
have served in important roles in the community.

The Hebrew word for priest, *kōhēn* (כֹּהֵן), conveys a unique
view of biblical priesthood. In Deuteronomy 18:1, God ap-
points some men from the tribe of Levi to serve as Israel's
priests (*kōhǎnîm*, the plural of *kōhēn*). The *kōhǎnîm* serve as
caretakers of the temple, perform rites and rituals, accept and
arrange tithes, and give offerings. Some Jewish scholars explain that there is a difference between a *kōhēn* (priest) and a

Levi (descendant of the tribe of Levi). *Kōhănîm* (priests) are also descended from the tribe of Levi, but they are descended from Aaron, the first high priest. Any other member of the tribe of Levi not descended from Aaron remains a Levi but never becomes a priest. The Levites wash the priests' hands and feet, but only priests can offer sacrifices.

Additionally, the biblical *kōhănîm* are unique in that they serve as an intermediary between God and the people of Israel. As we see in Deuteronomy 18:5, priests are called to "stand to minister in the name of the LORD." In the Jewish view, this role as intermediary between the people and God has a narrow scope. The priest is designated by God for service, but he has no unique authority over the people.

Numbers 18:22–23 gives us a summary of the role of the Levites: "And henceforth the children of Israel shall not come nigh the tent of meeting, lest they bear sin, and die. But the Levites alone shall do the service of the tent of meeting, and they shall bear their iniquity; it shall be a statute for ever throughout your generations, and among the children of Israel they shall have no inheritance." These verses refer to Levites in general, not specifically to the priests. Levites are given a clear role that the rest of the Israelites are precluded from doing.

kōhēn

כֹּהֵן

"priest"

Priest to God
—Genesis 14:18

Egyptian priests
—Genesis 47:22

Israelite priests
—Joshua 3:13

We see also in Numbers 18:20–21 that the Levites and Levitical priests are to live in dependence on others' giving for their material needs: "And the LORD said unto Aaron: 'Thou shalt have no inheritance in their land, neither shalt thou have any portion among them; I am thy portion and thine inheritance among the children of Israel. And unto the children of Levi, behold, I have given all the tithe in Israel for an inheritance, in return for their service which they serve, even the service of the tent of meeting.' " In ancient Israel, Levites (including the priests) are not allowed to own property and they share in "no inheritance" among their fellow Israelites. They are meant only to receive what they need from what is given to them.

In reflecting on the term *kōhēn*, it is possible to conclude that having unique responsibilities does not preclude the Levitical priests from depending on God and on the people they serve. This state of dependency perhaps deepens their relationship with God, as they learn to trust in his care for them, and helps them to better serve those who generously provide for their needs.

כֹּהֵן

מַעֲשֵׂר

ma'ăśēr

tithe

ma'ăśēr - מַעֲשֵׂר

עַשֵּׂר תְּעַשֵּׂר אֵת כָּל תְּבוּאַת זַרְעֶךָ
הַיֹּצֵא הַשָּׂדֶה שָׁנָה שָׁנָה

*"Thou shalt surely tithe all the increase of thy seed, that which is
brought forth in the field year by year."*
Deuteronomy 14:22

A common theme throughout the Bible is generosity.
God gives the Israelites a set of instructions in
Deuteronomy 15:7–11 that focuses on generosity toward
others. God says to them, "Therefore I command you, 'You
shall open wide your hand to your brother, to the needy and
to the poor' " (verse 11, ESV). They are told to give "freely"
to those in need and not allow their hearts to "be grudging"
when they give (verse 10, ESV).

In this context of God commanding the people of Israel
to give, we can more fully understand the biblical principles related to tithing. The Hebrew word for *he tithed*, '*iśśēr*
(עִשֵּׂר), literally means "he took a tenth." The root of the

word *ma'ăśēr* is *'eśer*
(עֶשֶׂר), meaning "ten."
In other words, tithes
are usually a tenth of
the whole. A derivative
word is *'iśśārôn*, mean-
ing "a tenth," as we see
in Leviticus 14:21.

There are three
types of biblical tithes.
The first tithe is given
by the Israelites to
the Levites, as seen in

ma'ăśēr

מַעֲשֵׂר

"tithe"

*Tithe given by the people of
Israel*
—Numbers 18:26

Take a tenth
—1 Samuel 8:14–15

Ten
—Genesis 24:55

Numbers 18:24. The second tithe is given by the Levites to
the higher priestly *kōhănîm*, who are descendants of Aaron
(Numbers 18:26–28). The third tithe is somewhat unusual
because it occurs only in the third year of a seven-year cycle
and is a more general offering to the poor (Deuteronomy
26:12). In these examples, we can see that the principle of
tithing—giving "a tenth" (*ma'ăśēr*)—is described in the biblical text as an expression of obedience and devotion to God.

The story of the Israelites seeking a king to rule over
them offers a different setting for the word *tithe* (*ma'ăśēr*).
In 1 Samuel 8:14–15, Samuel says to the people, "He [the
king] will take the best of your fields and vineyards and olive orchards and give them to his servants. He will take the
tenth of your grain and of your vineyards and give it to his
officers and to his servants" (ESV). In this example, the tithe
is taken by the king, apparently to finance military officers
and royal servants. This could be seen as something similar

to a tax for funding a government. But generosity, in the pure sense of the term, is not involved.

By contrast, sincere giving, according to various Bible passages, brings joy to those who show generosity. "Then the people rejoiced because they had given willingly, for with a whole heart they had offered freely to the LORD" (1 Chronicles 29:9, ESV).

מַעֲשֵׂר

מָשִׁיחַ

māšîaḥ

anointed one

māšîaḥ - מָשִׁיחַ

וַיֹּאמֶר יְהוָה קוּם מְשָׁחֵהוּ כִּי זֶה הוּא

"And the LORD said: 'Arise, anoint him; for this is he.' "
1 Samuel 16:12

The Bible often shows God enabling men and women to fulfill his purposes. For example, he calls and raises up Joseph from captivity and prison to save Israel from starvation during a famine (Genesis 37–47). Moses rescues the Israelites from slavery in Egypt (Exodus 2–14). Queen Esther, risking her own life, finds a way to prevent the annihilation of her people (the book of Esther). God calls Nehemiah to rebuild Jerusalem and its walls so that the returned exiles would have homes and security (the book of Nehemiah). There are many other examples.

These biblical stories show God setting different people apart for a specific purpose at a specific time in history. In 1 Samuel 16:12, we read about the moment when David is anointed as king over Israel. By understanding the Hebrew for the word *anointed*, it is possible to gain a more complete view of God's work through people.

The Hebrew word for *anointed* is *māšûaḥ* or *māšîaḥ* (מָשׁוּחַ or מָשִׁיחַ). It is also the Hebrew origin for the English word *messiah*; however, the Hebrew meaning of the word is not synonymous with the English usage. In fact, the Hebrew *māšîaḥ* ("anointed one" or "messiah") is used in many different contexts.

In the Bible, the terms *māšûaḥ* and *māšîaḥ* refer either to somebody anointed, such as a king or high priest, or to somebody great. For example, in Leviticus 4, *māšîaḥ* is used several times to describe an anointed priest. The word refers to a son or descendant of David in Psalm 132. And it is used in reference to Persian king Cyrus in Isaiah 45:1. In each of these cases, God sets a person apart for a purpose. The word *messiah* literally means "someone who is anointed," and refers to a savior. The Hebrew verb, however, can also be used for more mundane purposes, such as spreading an ointment or oil on one's body, or even spreading something—such as peanut butter on bread. It is not used exclusively for more elevated purposes.

Although the term *anointed* (*māšîaḥ*) is not used in Isaiah 11, many biblical scholars view this chapter as a

māšîaḥ

מָשִׁיחַ

"anointed one"

Smeared
—Jeremiah 22:14

Anointed
—Isaiah 45:1

Messiah
—Daniel 9:25

partial description of a messiah. Some Christian theologians believe the chapter points to Jesus as the Messiah. Many Jewish scholars believe it describes an ordinary person who will serve Israel in significant but non-supernatural ways.

Whatever the case, Isaiah 11 states that this messiah will accomplish the following: be a descendant of Jesse, David's father (verse 1); have the Spirit of God rest on him (verse 2); do justice for the poor (verse 4); put the wicked to death (verse 4); gather the exiles of Israel (verses 11–12); stop conflicts between Jews (verse 13); and destroy the enemies of Israel (verses 14–15).

Regardless of your viewpoint about a messiah, understanding how the Hebrew word *māšîaḥ* is used to describe God calling individuals to serve his purposes can be inspiring for any person hoping to make a contribution in the world. The biblical examples of people whom God anointed (*māšîaḥ*) to accomplish his goals in the world can perhaps serve as reminders for us that every person can make a significant contribution to the lives of those around them.

מָשִׁיחַ

מִשְׁפָּט

וּצְדָקָה

mišpāṭ ûṣədāqāh

justice and charity

mišpāṭ ûṣədāqāh - מִשְׁפָּט וּצְדָקָה
כֹּה אָמַר יְהוָה עֲשׂוּ מִשְׁפָּט וּצְדָקָה

"Thus saith the LORD: Execute ye justice and righteousness, and deliver the spoiled out of the hand of the oppressor; and do no wrong, do no violence, to the stranger, the fatherless, nor the widow, neither shed innocent blood in this place."

Jeremiah 22:3

Among the many debates surrounding government justice systems is the tension between making criminals pay fairly for their crimes and also caring for the victims of injustice. This tension can also be found in Jeremiah 22.

The phrase *mišpāṭ ûṣədāqāh* מִשְׁפָּט וּצְדָקָה ("justice and righteousness") occurs in Jeremiah 22:3. It is alternately translated as "judgment and righteousness" (KJV) and "what is just and right" (NIV). From the perspective of the Jewish tradition, however, perhaps the best translation of these words would be "justice and charity." These translations and many more all conflate the ideas of "charity" and "righteousness" as if they are interchangeable, when in fact they are not.

According to some Hebrew scholars, the word *righteousness* is not a correct translation for *ṣeḏāqāh*. *Righteousness* tends to fit easily into any place that the Hebrew for

mišpāṭ ûṣəḏāqāh

מִשְׁפָּט וּצְדָקָה

"justice and charity"

Justice and righteousness
—Jeremiah 22:3

Judgment and righteousness
—Jeremiah 22:3
(alternate meaning)

Something that is just and right
—Jeremiah 22:3
(alternate meaning)

charity might appear, which unfortunately opens the door to variances in translations.

However, Jeremiah 22:3 and its use of *ûṣəḏāqāh* ("and charity") conveys the tension between justice and charity. The verse affirms that justice should be carried out in a way that aids a victim of injustice and prevents harm to other citizens.

The Hebrew translation of "justice and charity" offers us an opportunity not found in other translations to gain insights about the tension between justice and charity. This is because the other translations convey words that are nearly synonymous—"justice and righteousness."

The concept of "justice and charity" stated by Jeremiah most likely would have been a revolutionary perspective in ancient times. Perhaps even today, the kinder face of justice—one that not only fairly punishes criminals but also cares for the victims—is sometimes difficult to encounter.

This verse can be seen as a reminder that punishing criminals fixes only half the problem, and that it is also important to consider the needs of victims and their communities.

מִשְׁפָּט
וּצְדָקָה

נַחֲלָה

naḥălāh

inheritance

naḥălāh - נַחֲלָה

וַיֹּאמֶר נָבוֹת אֶל־אַחְאָב חָלִילָה לִּי
מֵיהוָה מִתִּתִּי אֶת נַחֲלַת אֲבֹתַי לָךְ

*"And Naboth said to Ahab: 'The LORD forbid it me, that I
should give the inheritance of my fathers unto thee.' "*
1 Kings 21:3

The Hebrew word *naḥălāh* (נַחֲלָה) is one of the biblical
words for "property" or "inheritance," but its meaning
goes deeper than what is conveyed in the English translations.
Naḥălāh is more than just an inheritance or a property. For
the biblical people of Israel, it refers to an ancestral possession
that is handed down from generation to generation. In fact, if
land were sold to a different family, whenever the next jubilee
year (Leviticus 25) rolled around (they take place every fifty
years, see p. 162), the new owner would be required to return
it to the original family that owned it.

A commercial negotiation in the book of 1 Kings has
the potential to open our eyes to the biblical meaning of

129

ancestral possessions. In 1 Kings 21:1–4, King Ahab is trying to buy or barter for a vineyard owned by a man named Naboth. Ahab asks Naboth to give him his vineyard so the king can use it for a vegetable garden. In exchange, Ahab offers a better vineyard, or fair payment.

Despite Ahab's offers, Naboth refuses. Naboth says to Ahab in 1 Kings 21:3, "The LORD forbid it me, that I should give the inheritance of my fathers [*naḥălāṭ ʾăḇōtay* נַחֲלַת אֲבֹתַי] unto thee." This land means so much to Naboth—because of its connection to his forefathers—that he denies even a king's wishes. It is highly possible that Naboth suspects he will not get the property back in the year of jubilee. He is telling Ahab that he cannot sell the land forever, as God forbids it. Naboth's strong connection to his property can help us understand the meaning of *naḥălāh*. When Naboth says that his vineyard is tied to his forefathers, he is announcing that his land has a meaning that goes far beyond a property title. For Naboth, *naḥălāh* means his property is inseparable from his identity.

Naḥălāh is also used for things other than land, as we can see in the inheritance of the Levites. Numbers 18:20 relates *naḥălāh* to the higher priestly class of the kohenim, Levitical priests who are descended from Aaron: "And the LORD

naḥălāh

נַחֲלָה

"inheritance"

Inheritance of property
—Numbers 18:20

Inheritance of career
—Numbers 18:21

Ancestral land
—1 Kings 21:3

said unto Aaron: 'Thou shalt have no inheritance in their land, neither shalt thou have any portion among them; I am thy portion and thine inheritance among the children of Israel.'" For this priestly class, God is their *naḥălāh*. They possess certain tasks and rights, such as tithes and serving in the temple. They are also entitled to eat parts of some sacrifices, and these rights are handed down from generation to generation.

And for the Levites, Numbers 18:21 tells us that their *naḥălāh* is "all the tithe in Israel," a relational expression of the generosity of the people. Levites have different tasks, rights, and tithes. They also have the cities of refuge (Numbers 35:6). Again, these rights are handed down from generation to generation and so are referred to as *naḥălāh*.

These examples show *naḥălāh* to be something meaningful beyond material transactions for nothing more than monetary gain. It is possible even for us to apply these ideas about *naḥălāh* in the modern world. Our lives can perhaps be made better when our material possessions and heritages have a meaningful connection to our histories, families, and identities.

נַחֲלָה

נִחַם

niham

to find solace and comfort

niham - נִחַם

וַיִּנָּחֶם יְהוָה עַל־הָרָעָה אֲשֶׁר דִּבֶּר
לַעֲשׂוֹת לְעַמּוֹ

*"And the LORD repented of the evil which He said He would do
unto His people."*
Exodus 32:14

The words "repented of the evil" in Exodus 32:14 describe how God relents from bringing disaster on the Israelites for worshiping the golden calf. Another English translation of this verse is the following: "And the LORD relented from the disaster that he had spoken of bringing on his people" (ESV).

The context of the verse, in Exodus 32, is Moses ascending Mount Sinai to receive the Ten Commandments. In his absence, the people of Israel create a calf out of molten gold and begin to worship it. Because the people have "corrupted themselves" (Exodus 32:7, ESV), God contemplates their destruction. However, Moses pleads with God to pardon the nation (verses 11–13). God mercifully relents

(Exodus 32:14)—he reverses his original intentions.

The Hebrew word *wayyinnaḥēm* (וַיִּנָּחֶם) in this verse conveys a sense of regret that cannot be fully captured in the English word *relent*. The Hebrew root *niḥam* (נָחַם) is found in the ominous prelude to the

niḥam

נָחַם

"to find solace and comfort"

Reconsider
—Genesis 6:6

Be consoled
—Genesis 38:12

Console oneself through vengeance
—Isaiah 1:24

Flood during Noah's time (Genesis 6–9). In that time "the wickedness of man was great in the earth, and . . . every intention of the thoughts of this heart was only evil continually" (Genesis 6:5, ESV). Genesis 6:6 describes God's response to the evil in the hearts of humanity: "And the LORD regretted that he had made man on the earth, and it grieved him to his heart" (ESV).

The Hebrew root *niḥam* (נָחַם) in Genesis 6:6 refers to God's deep regret. We might conclude that God is so grieved by human decisions to pursue evil that he comes to a point of heartfelt grief. Nothing in these verses indicates that his regret is the result of some mistake he made in creating humanity. It is more likely that he laments the free-will decisions of people who turn away from him and follow evil paths.

We can gain an even richer understanding of the term *niḥam* by looking at Genesis 38:12: "And in process of time

Shua's daughter, the wife of Judah, died; and Judah was comforted [*niḥam*], and went up unto his sheep-shearers to Timnah, he and his friend Hirah the Adullamite." Here the word *niḥam* means "to find solace and comfort" in the aftermath of tragedy. This seems, at first glance, to be unrelated to the idea of *regret*, which usually means "to lament the past." By comparison, "finding solace" usually conveys the idea of *peace*. So, as we study these meanings closely, the duality of meaning in the word *niḥam* can be perplexing.

Looking more carefully at this unlikely association provides a fresh insight into the biblical idea of regret. From the Hebrew language, we can see that regret does not mean grieving endlessly about the past. Instead, regret can be seen as the first step to setting a new direction toward finding comfort or solace. In other words, true regret is possibly conveyed in *niḥam* as the doorway to solace. With this understanding, regret sets its eyes on the future and leads to solace (peace).

As we consider the word *niḥam*, with all its layers, it is reasonable to conclude that it implies accepting the past, with the pain and sadness that it carries, and finding comfort in looking ahead to the future. It seems to set forth the liberating idea that even with a painful past, one can find solace and thrive.

נָחַם

פֶּסַח

pesaḥ

to pass over

pesaḥ - פֶּסַח

וְהָיָה הַדָּם לָכֶם לְאֹת עַל הַבָּתִּים
אֲשֶׁר אַתֶּם שָׁם וְרָאִיתִי אֶת הַדָּם
וּפָסַחְתִּי עֲלֵכֶם

*"And the blood shall be to you for a token upon the houses where
ye are; and when I see the blood, I will pass over you, and there
shall no plague be upon you to destroy you, when I smite the land
of Egypt."*
Exodus 12:13

Although the Passover holiday is most widely known as
a Jewish commemoration of the Israelites' exodus from
Egypt, a closer look at the Hebrew word for Passover sheds
light on a foundational aspect of life: our choices between
right and wrong.

The word *pesaḥ* (פֶּסַח) refers to the festival of Passover, or
the offering given on that festival. Passover originates from
the story found in Exodus 12. As one of the plagues God

brings on the Egyptians, he smites all the firstborns in Egypt. However, God gives the Israelites instructions to follow so that their own children will be spared. They must sacrifice a baby sheep or goat, wipe its blood on their doorposts, eat it, and burn the leftovers—all on an appointed night.

The name for the Passover holiday is shown in Exodus 12:13: "And the blood shall be to you for a token upon the houses where ye are; and when I see the blood, I will pass over [*pesaḥ*] you, and there shall no plague be upon you to destroy you, when I smite the land of Egypt." The name *pesaḥ*, which usually means "to pass over," is derived from the Pascal lamb that was sacrificed and from the fact that God passed over the Israelites' homes that had been marked with blood.

A less common definition of *pesaḥ* can be seen in 1 Kings 18:21: "Elijah went before the people and said, 'How long will you waver [*pesaḥ*] between two opinions? If the LORD is God, follow him; but if Baal is God, follow him' " (NIV).

In this verse, the word *pesaḥ* means "to alternate" or "to waver." Elijah is asking people to choose between worshiping God and worshiping the god Baal.

In the Jewish tradition, there is a correlation between Elijah's question and the Passover. Elijah asks when

pesaḥ

פֶּסַח

"to pass over"

Pass over
—Exodus 12:13

The Passover lamb
—Exodus 12:11

To alternate/waver
—1 Kings 18:21

the people will stop wavering between faith in God and the idolatrous choice of Baal. During the Exodus, the people of Israel have to make a choice to obey God and trust in his protection of them.

Many choices we face each day often come down to a decision between what is right and wrong. And in those moments, making a clear choice for what is moral and right, rather than wavering, is the best path. The Passover story can perhaps serve as a reminder to find and choose the right path in our decisions. A life that consists of righteous decisions is a life to be venerated.

פֶּסַח

riḥam

compassion

riham - רְחַם

כְּרַחֵם אָב עַל־בָּנִים רִחַם יְהוָה
עַל־יְרֵאָיו

"Like as a father hath compassion upon his children,
So hath the LORD compassion upon them that fear Him."
Psalm 103:13

In May 1995, a young Hasidic girl from Brooklyn, New York, went missing in some woods for several days. Driven by compassion, about 1,000 volunteers searched the woods for the girl, including 600 bearded Hasidic men wearing traditional black attire. They came from New York, Montreal, Boston, and Washington, DC.

To everyone's relief, they found the girl on May 7. According to author Annie Dillard, a man named Isaac Fortgang explained why so many people had come to search for the girl. Stating his view of the Bible, he said: "It says in the Bible that to save a life is to save the entire world."[8]

This story depicts some elements of the Jewish notion

of God's love and compassion, as revealed in the Hebrew language. *Raḥămîm* (רַחֲמִים) is the Hebrew term that refers to compassion, and it often conveys God's love for humanity and the unique love that parents have for their children. The variants of the Hebrew root of the word, *riḥ*

am (רְחַם), express in biblical contexts an even deeper love of God than the English word *compassion* can convey.

The similar word *reḥem*, in its most literal sense, refers to a mother's womb. We can see a simple usage in Genesis 20:18: "For the LORD had fast closed up all the wombs [*reḥem* רֶחֶם] of the house of Abimelech, because of Sarah Abraham's wife." From literal uses like this, the figurative uses of the word have emerged.

There are numerous examples in the Bible of God speaking to people with the same vocabulary. For instance, Psalm 103:13–14 says, "Like as a father hath compassion [*kəraḥēm* כְּרַחֵם] upon his children, so hath the LORD compassion [*riḥam* רִחַם] upon them that fear him. For he knoweth our frame; he remembereth that we are dust." This conveys that *raḥămîm* is a type of compassion that is best known as coming from a parent toward a child.

Another verse reinforces this point. In Jeremiah 1:5 God says to the prophet Jeremiah, "Before I formed you in the womb I knew you, and before you were born ["emerged from the womb," *mēreḥem* מֵרֶחֶם], I consecrated you; I appointed you a prophet to the nations" (ESV). In this verse, we see God expressing his deep, personal affection toward Jeremiah, even when he was in the womb.

The remarkable compassion that the Hasidim showed when they searched for the lost Brooklyn girl perhaps could not compare to the even more profound love that the girl's parents had for their lost child. It is the love of that girl's parents that comes closest to what the term *riḥam* conveys about the heartfelt compassion of God for us. The Hebrew word informs us that God looks at his creation with the same feelings that parents have for a child.

David expresses this parent-child bond in Psalm 22:10–11: "For Thou art He that took me out of the womb; Thou madest me trust when I was upon my mother's breasts. Upon Thee I have been cast from my birth [*mērāḥem* מֵרֶחֶם]; Thou art my God from my mother's womb."

From this perspective, it is possible to perceive that God's compassion establishes a foundation for David's self-worth. Like David, we may benefit from focusing on God's compassionate nature and his love for humanity as a way to find joy and meaning in this life.

רְחַם

śāq

sackcloth

śāq - שָׂק

וַיִּקְרַע בְּגָדָיו וַיָּשֶׂם־שַׂק עַל־בְּשָׂרוֹ
וַיָּצוֹם וַיִּשְׁכַּב בַּשָּׂק וַיְהַלֵּךְ אַט

"He rent his clothes, and put sackcloth upon his flesh, and fasted,
and lay in sackcloth, and went softly."

1 Kings 21:27

M any people think that humility is related to weakness
and resignation, which often seems like a recipe for
failure in a competitive world. But, paradoxically, humility
can be seen as a powerful force for relational health.

What does it mean to be humble? Learning about a biblical garment can help us answer that question. The garment
is called sackcloth, or *śāq* (שָׂק), as it is called in Hebrew. It
was made from a rough, woven cloth, and the people of
Israel would wear it usually during times of mourning or
deep sorrow.

Sackcloth appears in the story of Ahab, a notorious-
ly wicked king of Israel (1 Kings 21:25–26). We read in

1 Kings 21:27 that Ahab heard a foreboding prophecy about God destroying his family line and then responded in sorrow and humility: "And when Ahab heard those words, he tore his clothes and put sackcloth on his flesh and fasted and lay in sackcloth and went about dejectedly" (ESV).

God's response to Ahab's sorrowful actions perhaps shows the benefits of humility. In verse 29, God tells Elijah, "Have you seen how Ahab has humbled himself before me? Because he has humbled himself before me, I will not bring the disaster in his days; but in his son's days I will bring the disaster upon his house" (ESV). In this biblical story, lives are spared because of Ahab's humility before God.

Another example of sackcloth occurs in the book of Esther when Mordecai hears that the Persian king had decreed the Jews to be killed (Esther 3:12–15). Esther 4:1 says, "When Mordecai learned all that had been done, Mordecai tore his clothes and put on sackcloth and ashes, and went out into the midst of the city, and he cried out with a loud and bitter cry" (ESV).

Esther 4:3 goes on to say: "And in every province, wherever the king's command and his decree reached, there was great mourning among the Jews, with fasting and weeping and lamenting, and many of them lay in sackcloth and ashes" (ESV).

śāq

שַׂק

"sackcloth"

A type of cloth worn to symbolize mourning
—1 Kings 21:25–27;
Esther 4:3

A sign of humility
—1 Kings 21:29

When comparing the motivations that prompt Mordecai and the Jews to wear sackcloth with the motivations of Ahab, we can see a significant similarity. Both wore sackcloth as an expression of their need for God's rescue. In both cases, wearing sackcloth can be seen as an outward demonstration of humility in their hearts. Both recognized their dependence on God—an admission that they cannot survive without him.

These examples using the Hebrew word *śāq* demonstrate a biblical principle that humility can be a powerful approach to dealing with problems. They also show that humility is an attitude of the heart and can result in positive outcomes.

סְגֻלָּה

səḡullāh

treasure

səgullāh - סְגֻלָּה

כִּי עַם קָדוֹשׁ אַתָּה לַיהוָה אֱלֹהֶיךָ בְּךָ
בָּחַר יְהוָה אֱלֹהֶיךָ לִהְיוֹת לוֹ לְעַם
סְגֻלָּה מִכֹּל הָעַמִּים אֲשֶׁר עַל פְּנֵי
הָאֲדָמָה

*"For thou art a holy people unto the Lord thy God: the Lord
thy God hath chosen thee to be His own treasure, out of all
peoples that are upon the face of the earth."*

Deuteronomy 7:6

Most people probably think of a chest full of gold
when they hear the word *treasure*. In the Bible, the
Hebrew word *səgullāh* סְגֻלָּה ("treasure") can refer to material
possessions or to people chosen by God. Just as kings look
to preserve and protect gold, precious jewels, and fine
craftsmanship for their enjoyment, God has declared that
he has chosen to preserve and protect Israel for his pleasure.

149

Aramaic texts reveal that the verbal form of this root (*s-g-l*) means "to heap up." The word *səḡullāh* is a passive noun—with the pattern *CəCuCCah*—meaning "that which is heaped up." Similarly, the root *y-r-š* means "to inherit" (see pages 198–201), while the noun form of that word (*yəruššāh*) means "that which is inherited."

səḡullāh

סְגֻלָּה

"treasure"

Literal treasure
—1 Chronicles 29:3

Prized possession
—Psalm 135:4

As many things in life, treasure comes with positives and negatives. King David willed his treasure (*səḡullāh*) to the temple of the Lord, which he knew his son Solomon would build. "Moreover also, because I have set my affection on the house of my God, seeing that I have a treasure [*səḡullāh*] of mine own of gold and silver, I give it unto the house of my God" (1 Chronicles 29:3). David's military and political successes had allowed him to amass ("heap up") a large amount of silver and gold during his reign. This allowed him to donate it to the temple yet to be built.

The writer of Ecclesiastes—named Qohelet (*qōhelet*) in Hebrew—takes a more negative view of treasure (*səḡullāh*). In reflecting on the futility of a multitude of earthly pursuits, he declares:

*I said in my heart: "Come now, I will try thee with mirth, and enjoy pleasure"; and, behold, this also was vanity. . . . I gathered me also silver and gold, and treasure [*səḡullāh*] . . .*

*and increased more than all that were before me in Jerusalem;
also my wisdom stood me instead. . . . Then I looked on all the
works that my hands had wrought, and on the labour that I
had laboured to do; and, behold, all was vanity and a striving
after wind, and there was no profit under the sun. (2:1–11)*

For Qohelet, treasure is not a worthwhile pursuit in and
of itself.

According to Psalm 135:4, God concerned himself with
protecting and preserving a people he would call his "own treasure" (Psalm 135:4). He even made a pact with Israel in this
regard. Israel was to be his treasure; and in turn, the people of
Israel were to obey God's commandments. "And the LORD has
declared today that you are a people for his treasured possession
[*səḡullāh*], as he has promised you, and that you are to keep all
his commandments" (Deuteronomy 26:18, ESV). The prophet
Malachi explained the outcome of this agreement for Israel.

*Then those who feared the LORD spoke with one another.
The LORD paid attention and heard them, and a book of
remembrance was written before him of those who feared
the Lord and esteemed his name. "They shall be mine, says
the LORD of hosts, in the day when I make up my treasured
possession [*səḡullāh*], and I will spare them as a man spares
his son who serves him." (3:16–17, ESV)*

As we consider the word *səḡullāh*, perhaps we might consider what we treasure and who treasures us.

סְגֻלָּה

שַׁבָּת

šabbaṯ

Sabbath

šabbat - שַׁבָּת

שֵׁשֶׁת יָמִים תֵּעָשֶׂה מְלָאכָה וּבַיּוֹם הַשְּׁבִיעִי שַׁבַּת שַׁבָּתוֹן

"Six days shall work be done; but on the seventh day is a sabbath of solemn rest, a holy convocation; ye shall do no manner of work; it is a sabbath unto the LORD in all your dwellings."
Leviticus 23:3

The concept of the Sabbath—a time to stop working and to focus on God—first appears in the Bible in Genesis 2:3. "So God blessed the seventh day and made it holy, because on it God rested from all his work that he had done in creation" (ESV). The holiness of the day is also conveyed in Leviticus 23:3. And the same pattern is given in Exodus 20:9–11, when God gives the people of Israel the Ten Commandments and tells them to remember the Sabbath as holy.

Studying the Hebrew word for *Sabbath*, *šabbat* (שַׁבָּת), can deepen our understanding of the concept of rest in the

Bible. In addition to defining the weekly day of rest, the word *šabbat* is used to describe the period of rest that occurs in the seven-year agricultural cycle described in Leviticus 25:2–7. In this farming cycle, God commands that every seventh year, called *šəmittāh* (שְׁמִטָּה), the land shall lie fallow and that no plowing, planting, and harvesting shall be performed.

Not only is *šabbat* the Sabbath day, but its verb form, *šābat* (שָׁבַת), means that God rested and desisted from work, as we see in Genesis 2:3. In Leviticus 23:3 we see another construct form, *šabbat šabbatôn*. This means a Sabbath of extended rest, and the double usage is also used for emphasis in several verses in the Bible. It is applied to the Sabbath in the verses above, to the Day of Atonement in Leviticus 16:30–31 and 23:32, and to the *šəmittāh* ("remission") year in Leviticus 25:4.

Based on these biblical texts, absolutely no work is permitted for the people of Israel on the Sabbath or on the Day of Atonement; and no work of any agricultural nature is permitted during the last year of a seven-year cycle. This is why Orthodox Jews do not drive on the Sabbath, for instance, as that would involve lighting a spark. Avoiding driving on the Sabbath

šabbat

שֶׁבֶת

"Sabbath"

Rest
—Genesis 2:3

Sabbath day
—Leviticus 23:2–3

Seventh year
—Leviticus 25:2

also gives them a proper day of rest. No radio, television, or travel means quality time at home with the family.

In the weekly *šabbat* and in the *šəmiṭṭāh* year, the biblical pattern of work and rest is seen as cyclical. A distinct period of work is followed by a defined period of rest, and then the cycle repeats. However, the meaning of the Hebrew *šabbat* is about more than mere idleness. The word conveys the idea that the rest period is holy, indicating that there is a spiritual element involved.

On this point, the study of the word *šabbat* might help us consider this spiritual dimension of the Sabbath. To comply with the agricultural year of rest (*šəmiṭṭāh*), the worker must place self-reliance in the background and trust God to provide while the land is dormant. The Sabbath, therefore, can be seen in the Bible as way of helping the people of Israel to consider God as the ultimate source of their provision.

Many people today find it difficult to rest. Electronic devices keep us tethered to work. Fear of losing jobs in a competitive economy keeps some people from using vacation time. And financial pressures might force many families to work longer hours. As we reflect on the biblical word *šabbat*, perhaps we can better assess the work-rest patterns in our lives and adjust as needed.

שַׁבָּת

שָׁלוֹם

šālôm

peace

šālôm - שָׁלוֹם

אֵין־מְתֹם בִּבְשָׂרִי מִפְּנֵי זַעְמֶךָ
אֵין־שָׁלוֹם בַּעֲצָמַי מִפְּנֵי חַטָּאתִי

*"There is no soundness in my flesh because of Thine indignation;
neither is there any health in my bones because of my sin."*
Psalm 38:4

What does peace mean to you? The word *šālôm* (שָׁלוֹם) is a familiar word in much of the West, and it is almost always translated as *peace* and recognized as a type of greeting. However, in the Bible, the word *šālôm* and its root do not always mean what the word *peace* means in English.

Šālôm often means "a cessation from war" or "a state of tranquility," which are the usual English connotations of the word. Joshua 9:15, an example of the former, says, "And Joshua made peace with them and made a covenant with them, to let them live" (ESV). In Psalm 4:8, an example of the latter, David says, "In peace I will both lie down and sleep; for you alone, O LORD, make me dwell in safety" (ESV).

The root of the word *šālôm* is often used to denote something as being complete and sound. Two verses related to building the temple in Jerusalem exhibit this well. The first is 1 Kings 7:51: "Thus all the work that king Solomon wrought in the house of the LORD was finished [*wattišlam* וַתִּשְׁלַם]

šālôm

שָׁלוֹם

"peace"

Peace
—Joshua 9:15

Soundness
—Job 9:4

Completeness
—1 Kings 7:51

A greeting
—Modern Hebrew usage

]." The second is 1 Kings 9:25: "And three times in a year did Solomon offer burnt-offerings and peace-offerings upon the altar which he built unto the LORD, offering thereby, upon the altar that was before the LORD. So he finished [*wəšillam* וְשִׁלַּם] the house."

Another use of the word *šālôm* that would not be obvious in English is the idea of "remaining intact." Job 9:4 speaks of God's power: "He is wise in heart, and mighty in strength; who hath hardened himself against Him, and prospered?" Here Job rhetorically asks if anyone can stand against God and prosper (or "remain intact"). The idea of remaining in one piece reinforces the previous definition of "completeness."

Interestingly, the phrase for "How are you?" in Hebrew—*Māh šəlômkāh?*—literally means "How is your completion?" In the Jewish tradition, a person missing a limb or an artery is considered incomplete. So in this context

158

šālēm / *šālôm* also means "complete." In other words, *māh šəlōmkāh?* means "How are you? Is everything okay?"

In Hebrew, *šālôm* is also used as one of the LORD's names. According to most Jewish scholars, God is given the title because he sustains the entire universe and keeps it together—or complete.

These examples of the different meanings of *šālôm* show how completeness and peace are related. The biblical usages of the word *šālôm* demonstrate something that is complete and not fractured. This presents us with a more profound understanding of the word *peace*.

שָׁלוֹם

שְׁנַת
הַיּוֹבֵל

šənaṯ hayyôḇēl

year of jubilee

šənaṯ hayyôḇēl - שְׁנַת הַיּוֹבֵל

וְקִדַּשְׁתֶּם אֵת שְׁנַת הַחֲמִשִּׁים שָׁנָה
וּקְרָאתֶם דְּרוֹר בָּאָרֶץ לְכָל־יֹשְׁבֶיהָ יוֹבֵל
הוא תִּהְיֶה לָכֶם וְשַׁבְתֶּם אִישׁ אֶל־אֲחֻזָּתוֹ
וְאִישׁ אֶל־מִשְׁפַּחְתּוֹ תָּשֻׁבוּ

"And ye shall hallow the fiftieth year, and proclaim liberty throughout the land unto all the inhabitants thereof; it shall be a jubilee unto you; and ye shall return every man unto his possession, and ye shall return every man unto his family."
Leviticus 25:10

E very person and family needs some form of capital to grow economically and to avoid poverty. But sometimes hard times—an economic crisis, a health problem, unemployment—can cause people to lose the capital they have built. What if there were a way to protect this capital from long-term loss?

The biblical "year of jubilee" (Leviticus 25:13), called in Hebrew a *šǝnaṯ hayyôḇēl*, serves exactly that purpose, even as it also carries deep spiritual significance. The phrase *šǝnaṯ hayyôḇēl* appears frequently in Leviticus 25 and 27. *Šǝnaṯ* literally means "year of." The word *yôḇēl* literally means a "ram" and appears in Joshua 6:5: "And when they make a long blast with the ram's [*yôḇēl*] horn . . . then all the people shall shout . . . and the wall of the city will fall down flat" (ESV). The "year of the ram" (*šǝnaṯ hayyôḇēl*) was the year of remission (of debts) in Israel. Scholars believe that the name stems from the practice of inaugurating this special year with the blowing of the ram's horn. The English rendering of this phrase as the "year of jubilee" comes from the transcription of this Hebrew word into Latin characters—*anno iobelei*. Our common English word *jubilation*, which describes the act of rejoicing, ultimately traces back to this Hebrew word and the joy associated with the cancelation of debts.

Leviticus 25 explains that this jubilee year involved more than just a cancellation of the debts involved with simple loans. Individuals who had been sold into slavery to pay off their debts were set free. Any family land sold outside the family was returned to that original family. In the book of Numbers, God had assigned the lots of

šǝnaṯ hayyôḇēl

שְׁנַת הַיּוֹבֵל

"year of jubilee"

Jubilee year
—Leviticus 25:13

Year of the ram's horn
—alternate meaning

land throughout Israel to specific tribes and families, making each tribe God's tenant. This practice of the jubilee year was an attempt to preserve those divine allotments. According to Leviticus 25, God said, "The land shall not be sold in perpetuity, for the land is mine. For you are strangers and sojourners with me" (verse 23, ESV).

But in conjunction with this financial relief was a challenge to trust in the provision of God. During this year of jubilee, farmers could not work in their fields but had to let them grow wild. They were forbidden from engineering their food supply themselves during this year and instead had to trust in God to provide food from the land. During that year landowners, field-workers, and slaves were all equally dependent upon God for their food, and no one could claim exclusive ownership of what grew on the land.

During the year of jubilee, the people of Israel were asked to focus on God's gifts and his acts of restoring the fortunes of families and individuals. The year served as a reminder that God is capable of providing for the daily needs of his people.

שְׁנַת
הַיּוֹבֵל

שְׁאוֹל

šə'ôl

the grave

šə'ôl - שְׁאוֹל

כִּי אֵין בַּמָּוֶת זִכְרֶךָ בִּשְׁאוֹל מִי יוֹדֶה־לָּךְ

"For in death there is no remembrance of Thee; in the nether-world
who will give Thee thanks?"
Psalm 6:6

Most people don't like to spend much time thinking about death, but the Bible's writers do not avoid the matter. By studying some of the biblical references about death, including the Hebrew word *šə'ôl*, we can broaden our understanding of what to many is an uncomfortable but inevitable fact of life.

She'ol שְׁאוֹל ("the grave," "the underworld," "the nether-world") is a difficult word to understand from the biblical usage. It has no clear Hebrew root, but its use in the Bible is common.

David conveys his idea of *šə'ôl* in relation to his constant struggle to escape death. In Psalm 6, David says of God, "For in death there is no remembrance of you; in Sheol who will give you praise?" (verse 5, ESV). In this verse, David appears to equate *šə'ôl* with physical death. In Psalm 16:10, David says to God, "For you will not abandon my soul to Sheol, or let your holy one see corruption" (ESV). In this verse, too, David uses *šə'ôl* to express the grave.

This simple use of the word *šə'ôl* to describe death and the grave is also present in Numbers 16:31–34, where we read about a group of people who oppose God and Moses. Because of their prideful rebellion, the ground splits open and "swallows" them. "So they and all that belonged to them went down alive into Sheol, and the earth closed over them" (verse 33, ESV).

šə'ôl

שְׁאוֹל

"the grave"

The underworld
—Numbers 16:33

The grave
—Psalm 16:10

Death
—Psalm 6:5

In numerous psalms, however, the psalmist states his belief that God will rescue his soul from *šə'ôl*. For example, in Psalm 49:15, the psalmist says, "But God will ransom my soul from the power of Sheol, for he will receive me" (ESV). And in Psalm 86:13, David writes, "For great is your steadfast love toward me; you have delivered my soul from the depths of Sheol" (ESV).

Verses like these that use the term *šə'ôl* often generate discussions about biblical views of death and about the theme of an eventual resurrection. For example, Isaiah 26:19 notes what appears to be a resurrection, saying, "Your dead shall live; their bodies shall rise. You who dwell in the dust, awake and sing for joy! For your dew is a dew of light, and the earth will give birth to the dead" (ESV).

Isaiah's thoughts here seem to describe *šə'ôl* as a temporary situation. This perspective also appears to be shared by Daniel, who says, "And many of them that sleep in the dust of the earth shall awake, some to everlasting life, and some to reproaches and everlasting abhorrence" (Daniel 12:2).

Some people believe Daniel is implying in this verse the idea of heaven and hell—the belief that permanent places exist to separate the good from the bad. Such a view of Daniel 12:2 might lead some to consider *šə'ôl* as a waystation or purgatory for the dead on their way to a permanent situation. However, that perspective is not explicitly stated in this verse. The verse simply describes a separation by which some experience "everlasting life" and others experience "everlasting abhorrence."

Death and eternity remain as mysterious topics within the pages of the Bible. For this reason, it is probably wise to not base our views on a single verse. Perhaps reading these few references about *šə'ôl* in the Bible might encourage you to study such matters more thoroughly.

שְׁאוֹל

שְׁאֵרִית

šəʾērîṯ

remnant

šə'ērît - שְׁאֵרִית

שִׂמְחָה וְצַהֲלוּ בְּרֹאשׁ הַגּוֹיִם הַשְׁמִיעוּ
הַלְלוּ וְאִמְרוּ הוֹשַׁע יְהוָה אֶת־עַמְּךָ אֵת
שְׁאֵרִית יִשְׂרָאֵל

*"Sing with gladness for Jacob, and shout at the head of the
nations; announce ye, praise ye, and say: 'O LORD, save Thy
people, the remnant of Israel.'"*
Jeremiah 31:7

In detective stories and television shows, the investigators
are often on the lookout for "remnants." These are pieces
of anything left behind at a crime scene that serve as clues.
These "remnants" have some connection to someone or
something that has been there in the past but is no longer
there. That past connection is key for the investigators.

When biblical authors wrote about a remnant, they typically used the word *šə'ērît*; and just like in the crime dra-
mas, the key characteristic of the *šə'ērît* is its connection to

the past. The first mention of a "remnant" (*šə'ērît*) in the Bible comes from the mouth of Joseph. After being sold into slavery by his brothers and obtaining a prominent place in Egyptian politics through a dizzying series of circumstances, Joseph explains to his brothers the purpose for the travails in his life (Genesis 45:7). He is now in a position to ensure that a "remnant" (*šə'ērît*) survives from the family of Jacob (also called Israel). The survival of Joseph and his brothers in Egypt is the only thing that provides the connection between the people Moses leads out of Egypt and the patriarchs: Abraham, Isaac, and Jacob.

This term "remnant" (*šə'ērît*) only appears in the Bible when there exists the threat of extinction. On a smaller scale, such a fear of extinction of the family line was very real for couples. A related term appears in the statement of the prophetess from Tekoa in her conversation with King David: "Thus they would quench my coal that is left and leave to my husband neither name nor remnant [*niš'ārāh*] on the face of the earth" (2 Samuel 14:7, ESV).

On a more national scale, the most common use of this term in the Bible is for the group of Judeans who continue to occupy the land after the Babylonian exile. There was a palpable and legitimate fear among the Judeans that the exile would

šə'ērît

שְׁאֵרִית

"remnant"

A remaining number of a population
—Jeremiah 31:7

Refuge
—Genesis 45:7

Remain behind
—Exodus 10:26

wipe out their ethnic identity, since they had seen this happen with the northern Israelite tribes in conjunction with the Assyrians. Would there be any legitimate connection between the people of Abraham, Moses, King David, Elijah, Micah, and Isaiah and the people living in the land of Israel?

Amos had prophesied that God would cut off the remnant of the Philistines, whom Samson and King David had battled. God's words in Amos 1:8 warned there would no longer exist any connection between any people group and the Philistines of old: "I will cut off the inhabitant from Ashdod, and him that holdeth the scepter from Ashkelon; I will turn My hand against Ekron, and the remnant [šəʾērîṯ] of the Philistines shall perish."

Therefore, the prophets and the people prayed to God that he would preserve their fragile remnant. The prophet Jeremiah was in the thick of it when Nebuchadnezzar and the Babylonians attacked Judah and Jerusalem. But he survived the ordeal, living out his days in Egypt. In the aftermath, he declared joyously: "Sing with gladness for Jacob, and shout at the head of the nations; announce ye, praise ye, and say: 'O LORD, save Thy people, the remnant [šəʾērîṯ] of Israel' " (Jeremiah 31:7). This prophetic message represents the gratitude that a remnant remains along with a prayer that it not be snuffed out.

This discussion of the word šəʾērîṯ ("remnant") and related terms provides a good opportunity to reflect on how our faith in God connects with that of those who have gone before us.

שְׁאֵרִית

שִׁבְטְךָ

וּמִשְׁעַנְתֶּךָ

šibṭəkā ûmišʿanteḵā

your rod and your staff

šibṭəkā ûmišʿantekā -
שִׁבְטְךָ וּמִשְׁעַנְתֶּךָ

גַּם כִּי אֵלֵךְ בְּגֵיא צַלְמָוֶת לֹא אִירָא
רָע כִּי אַתָּה עִמָּדִי שִׁבְטְךָ וּמִשְׁעַנְתֶּךָ
הֵמָּה יְנַחֲמֻנִי

"Yea, though I walk through the valley of the shadow of death,
I will fear no evil, for Thou art with me;
Thy rod and Thy staff, they comfort me."
Psalm 23:4

In a high-pressure, fast-paced world, many people struggle with anxiety and worry. Perhaps for this reason, Psalm 23 is so well known and enjoyed today. In it, we see King David sharing what he's learned about overcoming fear. And as one who in his youth tended sheep, he writes this psalm using the metaphor of a shepherd caring for his flock.

The phrase *šibṭəkā ûmišʿantekā* שִׁבְטְךָ וּמִשְׁעַנְתֶּךָ ("your

173

rod and your staff") appears in Psalm 23:4. The difference between a rod and a staff sounds minor in English, but the Hebrew words have different meanings. The Hebrew word for *rod* is *šēbeṭ* (שֵׁבֶט). In Genesis 49:10, this word refers to a scepter, a symbol of authority: "The scepter shall not

šibṭəkā ûmišʿanteka

שִׁבְטְךָ וּמִשְׁעַנְתֶּךָ

"your rod and your staff"

Rod and staff
—Psalm 23:4

Scepter and support
—alternate translation

God's control and God's support
—Psalm 23:4

depart from Judah, nor the ruler's staff from between his feet, until tribute comes to him; and to him shall be the obedience of the peoples" (ESV).

A staff has a completely different Hebrew meaning. The Hebrew word for *staff* in Psalm 23:4 is *mašʿēnāh* (מַשְׁעֵנָה). This word comes from the root *šāʿan* (שָׁעַן), which means "support." Zechariah 8:4 says, "Thus saith the Lord of hosts: There shall yet old men and old women sit in the broad places of Jerusalem, every man with his staff in his hand for very age." There are other uses of *mašʿēnāh* in the Bible, but none of them contradict the word's simple meaning of "support."

David's statement in Psalm 23 takes on a richer meaning when we understand the Hebrew connotations—that a *rod* refers to a scepter and that a *staff* offers support. David appears to be saying in verse 4 that he is comforted by God's rule and support in his life.

This perspective can be carried into an interpretation of Psalm 23:5: "Thou preparest a table before me in the presence of mine enemies." This might be seen as a restatement of the previous verse but applied to the real world, which is full of threats that cause fear and anxiety. From this viewpoint, God's rod signifies his authority over even the wicked who pursue David, and David is supported through his trials by God's comforting staff.

As we consider this popular psalm and the meanings of *rod* and *staff*, perhaps we can reflect on how David is expressing his complete trust in God. The comfort that David receives from God's rod and staff alleviates his fears of worldly threats and evils.

שִׁבְטְךָ
וּמִשְׁעַנְתֶּךָ

טָמֵא

ṭāmēʾ

unclean

tāmē' - טָמֵא

וָאֹמַר אוֹי־לִי כִּי־נִדְמֵיתִי כִּי אִישׁ
טְמֵא־שְׂפָתַיִם אָנֹכִי וּבְתוֹךְ עַם־טְמֵא
שְׂפָתַיִם אָנֹכִי יוֹשֵׁב כִּי אֶת־הַמֶּלֶךְ יְהוָה
צְבָאוֹת רָאוּ עֵינָי

"Then said I: Woe is me! for I am undone; because I am a man of unclean lips, and I dwell in the midst of a people of unclean lips; for mine eyes have seen the King, the LORD of hosts."
Isaiah 6:5

I n Isaiah 6, the prophet Isaiah shares about an awesome encounter with a holy God, which leads him to humbly admit that he and his people have "unclean lips"—a reference to their sinfulness. His direct experience with God's holiness makes him feel an ominous sense of "woe."

To better understand what Isaiah is experiencing in this story, it can be helpful to look closely at the meaning of the Hebrew adjective *ṭāmē'* (טָמֵא). The term *ṭāmē'* describes a ritual uncleanliness for the people of Israel that required isolation and immersion in natural water for its removal. The word *ṭāmē'* is used in numerous contexts throughout the Bible. Exploring them can enrich our understanding of what Isaiah experiences with God.

Leviticus 11:4–7 refers to different animals that the Israelites should not to eat because they are considered "unclean" (*ṭāmē'*). Numbers 19:16 states that a person is *ṭāmē'* for seven days when they have various types of contact with the dead. Ezekiel 22:3–5 refers to a city that has "defiled" itself (verb form of *ṭāmē'*—לְטָמְאָה *ləṭāmə'āh*) through idolatrous practices. These are only a few ways that a person or society might become *ṭāmē'* according to the Hebrew Bible. But in all of these cases, the word *ṭāmē'* conveys a state of spiritual uncleanliness in relation to a holy God.

The noun form of the word *ṭāmē'* is *ṭum'āh*, meaning "uncleanliness." According to some Hebrew scholars, there are different levels of *ṭum'āh*—including touching an idol, practicing idolatry, being with menstruating women, touching a dead person, and speaking badly of other people. Isaiah becomes aware of his *ṭum'āh* during his encounter with God, when the

ṭāmē'

טָמֵא

"unclean"

Ritual impurity
—Numbers 19:16

Defiled
—Ezekiel 22:3–5

Nonkosher
—Leviticus 11:4–7

prophet sees the throne of God and the seraphim (Isaiah 6:2). And then, being overwhelmed by God's holiness, he realizes that he is full of sin. All he can say is, "Woe is me! for I am undone." His pride is defeated.

God does not leave Isaiah wallowing in his impurity; nor does he cast Isaiah aside. Instead, God steps in to purify and save the humbled Isaiah, as we see in Isaiah 6:6–7. A seraph comes to Isaiah "with a glowing stone in his hand" and touches the hot stone to Isaiah's mouth. The seraph says, "Behold, this has touched your lips; your guilt is taken away, and your sin atoned for" (ESV).

Isaiah's condition of *ṭum'āh* is purified by God. This is followed by God giving Isaiah the role of a prophet (Isaiah 6:8–9). We see in these verses that the forgiveness provided by God frees Isaiah to serve him. His *ṭum'āh* is not the end of his story.

The pattern that emerges from Isaiah's life—his encounter with God's holiness, his woeful state of impurity, the restoring forgiveness of God, and his renewed purpose in life—can perhaps be seen as a hopeful way of seeing our own lives.

טָמֵא

תְּפִלָּה

təpp̄illāh

prayer

təpillāh - תְּפִלָּה

כִּי בֵיתִ֔י בֵּית־תְּפִלָּה יִקָּרֵא לְכָל־הָעַמִּים

*"For My house shall be called a house of prayer
for all peoples."*
Isaiah 56:7

Many people struggle with questions about prayer. There is the busyness of life, and there are distractions. Despite the common obstacles to prayer, Isaiah 56:7 shows us that God opens the doors of his house to "all peoples" to pray.

As Isaiah is writing this chapter, people are using the temple in Jerusalem as a place for prayer. The ancient temple, he explains, is not intended as an exclusive club with membership reserved for the Jewish people; it is a universal house of prayer for people of all nations.

The Bible generally refers to the temple as a tabernacle, or in Hebrew *miškan haššēm* (מִשְׁכַּן יְהוָה), or God's dwelling

181

place (Numbers 16:9). This term implies that the temple is primarily a place to "appear before the Lord God" (Exodus 23:17). These verses appear to indicate that prayer is about intimacy with God.

To gain a deeper appreciation of prayer, a better understanding of the Hebrew word

təp̄illāh

תְּפִלָּה

"prayer"

Prayer
—Isaiah 56:7

Entreat
—1 Samuel 1:27

Interpose/Intervene
—Psalm 106:30

used by Isaiah for prayer, *təp̄illāh* (תְּפִלָּה), can be helpful. The word *təp̄illāh* comes from the root *pillēl* (פִּלֵּל), meaning "to entreat." It is used in the word *hitpallēl*, which means to "entreat oneself." According to this etymology, prayer is seen to be an introspection, a reflection on one's self in relation to God.

However, sometimes the world's influence in our lives might inhibit our awareness of God. This is one reason why prayer can be helpful in life. Many people find that prayer is a way of including God's perspectives in our decisions, and of deepening our relationships with God, and of evaluating our moral conditions. King David wrote in prayer: "Search me, O God, and know my heart! Try me and know my thoughts! And see if there be any grievous way in me, and lead me in the way everlasting" (Psalm 139:23–24, ESV).

This understanding of *təp̄illāh* also affords us some insight into the idea of the "house of prayer" spoken of by

Isaiah. The inclusive nature of the temple, as described by Isaiah, implies that God listens to all prayers. As the medieval Jewish philosopher Judah HaLevi explains in his work *The Kuzari*, the temple imposes limits on the material world, drawing people into God's dwelling place.[9] This is often seen by Jewish people as God's design for self-reflection—not in isolation, but in the presence of God.

תְּפִלָּה

תּוֹרָה

tôrāh

law

tôrāh - תּוֹרָה

וַיִּכְתֹּב מֹשֶׁה אֶת־הַתּוֹרָה הַזֹּאת

"And Moses wrote this law."
Deuteronomy 31:9

What is the Torah—the "law" that Moses wrote, according to Deuteronomy 31:9? The word *tôrāh* תּוֹרָה ("instruction" or "law") appears hundreds of times in the Bible and can be used to refer to anything from the first five books of the Bible to the entire Bible, and even to all teachings from God. The most common usage of it in the Bible is in reference to instruction from God.

In Deuteronomy 31:12, Moses tells the people of Israel, "Assemble the people, the men and the women and the little ones, and thy stranger that is within thy gates, that they may hear, and that they may learn, and fear the LORD your God, and observe to do all the words of this law." The verse refers to "this law [*tôrāh*]." The Torah in this context refers specifically to the five books of Moses, as the rest of the Bible had not been written yet.

Though the term *tôrāh* is generally used in Hebrew to refer to the five books of Moses, the Jews also have what they refer to as an "Oral Torah," which refers to later expounding and explanations, handed down orally through generations. These became the Mishnah and the Talmud, as they were codified at a later date. In English, the term *Bible* also includes the Prophets and the Writings, not just the Pentateuch (the first five books of the Bible), and so the Bible is not just the Torah, although it is also considered by many to be holy.

Deuteronomy 31:9 says, "And Moses wrote this law [*tôrāh*], and delivered it unto the priests the sons of Levi, that bore the ark of the covenant of the LORD, and unto all the elders of Israel." But in the next verses, Moses makes it clear that every seven years he wants "all Israel" to hear God's law read to them, not just the priests (Deuteronomy 31:10–11). Based on this reference, it appears God doesn't want his law and commandments to be held solely by religious leaders. Moses seeks to make certain that this would not be the case.

Moreover, Deuteronomy 31:12 indicates that God also wants the "men and the women and the little ones" as well as the "stranger" to observe the Torah. This might be seen as an expression of inclusiveness, a desire to see all people benefit from

tôrāh

תּוֹרָה

"law"

God's instruction
—Deuteronomy 31:9

Instruction
—Proverbs 1:8

God's law
—Exodus 12:49

God's wisdom. Regardless of sex, age, and nationality, Moses wanted the Torah to be heard by all Israelites and the foreigners with them.

The psalmist who wrote Psalm 119 expressed a deep love for God's law (*tôrāh*): "Oh how I love your law! It is my meditation all the day. Your commandment makes me wiser than my enemies, for it is ever with me" (verses 97–98, ESV). These words, and the words in Deuteronomy 31, show a deep reverence for God's instruction. They also reveal a belief that God's law—the *tôrāh*—is filled with wisdom for all people.

תּוֹרָה

וּמָל יהוה
אֱלֹהֶיךָ אֵת
לְבָבְךָ

ûmāl haššēm ʾĕlōheykā
ʾet̲ ləb̲āb̲k̲ā

God will circumcise your heart

ûmāl haśśēm ʾĕlōheykā
ʾet ləbābkā -

וּמָל יְהוָה אֱלֹהֶיךָ אֵת לְבָבְךָ

וּמָל יְהוָה אֱלֹהֶיךָ אֶת־לְבָבְךָ וְאֶת־לְבַב
זַרְעֶךָ לְאַהֲבָה אֶת־יְהוָה אֱלֹהֶיךָ
בְּכָל־לְבָבְךָ וּבְכָל־נַפְשְׁךָ לְמַעַן חַיֶּיךָ

*"And the LORD thy God will circumcise thy heart, and the
heart of thy seed, to love the LORD thy God with all thy heart,
and with all thy soul, that thou mayest live."*
Deuteronomy 30:6

The phrase from Deuteronomy 30:6 "And the LORD thy
God will circumcise thy heart" (*ûmāl haśśēm ʾĕlōheykā
ʾet ləbābkā*) is, for many people, rather strange. It can be
difficult to understand what it means to have a circumcised
heart. Although circumcision generally describes a physical

189

operation on male genitalia, it can also be used as an allegory, as we see in this verse. Many Hebrew scholars explain this allegory to mean that circumcision of the heart requires no physical action. On the contrary, it involves repentance and resisting temptation. Once a person repents,

ûmāl haššēm ʾĕlōheykā ʾeṭ ləḇāḇkā

וּמָל יְהוָה אֱלֹהֶיךָ אֶת לְבָבְךָ

"God will circumcise your heart"

Circumcision of the heart (literal)
—Deuteronomy 30:6

Make you capable of loving God
—Deuteronomy 30:6

Make yourself worthy of living
—Deuteronomy 10:16

God circumcises the heart and removes temptation altogether.

Circumcision of the heart could perhaps point to a more emotional covenant with God. The phrase is open to interpretations, but added context can improve our understanding of this important issue.

First, we can look at another example showing the opposite of a circumcised heart: the hardening of Pharaoh's heart. Two verses offer a full view of what is occurring in his life. Exodus 7:3 says that *God* will harden Pharaoh's heart, but Exodus 8:28 says, "Pharaoh hardened his heart this time also, and he did not let the people go." God hardens Pharaoh's heart in the former, and Pharaoh hardens his own heart in the latter. There are many interpretations of these verses, but both convey the notion that Pharaoh will continue to reject God's will to free the Israelites.

In Deuteronomy 10:16, Moses tells the Israelites to humble themselves and follow God by obeying his commandments. He says, "Circumcise therefore the foreskin of your heart, and be no longer stubborn" (ESV). Here we find the circumcising of the heart leading to an openness to submitting to God's will. This is quite different from what we read about the hardening of Pharaoh's heart, which leads him to complete stubborness in relation to God's will.

With all of this in mind, it might be easier to grasp the meaning of circumcising the heart. The phrase seems to indicate a person's willingness to accept the will of God and reject stubbornness. Perhaps it is important to remember the consequences in Pharaoh's life as a result of his refusal to soften his heart before God. His stubbornness leads his nation into extensive suffering under all the plagues described in Exodus 7–12.

By contrast, biblical references such as Deuteronomy 30:6 speak of the benefits of a circumcised heart, which leads to God's goodness. In your view, what role does the human heart play in the health and flourishing of our lives?

וּמָל יְהוָה
אֱלֹהֶיךָ אֶת
לְבָבְךָ

191

וְנָטְע֖וּ

כְרָמִים֙ וְשָׁת֣וּ

אֶת־יֵינָ֑ם

wənaṭʿû kərāmîm
wəšāṯû ʾeṯ yênām

*and they shall plant vineyards and
drink their wine*

wənaṭʿû kərāmîm wəšāṯû
ʾeṯ yênām -

וְנָטְעוּ כְרָמִים וְשָׁתוּ אֶת־יֵינָם

וְשַׁבְתִּי אֶת־שְׁבוּת עַמִּי יִשְׂרָאֵל וּבָנוּ
עָרִים נְשַׁמּוֹת וְיָשָׁבוּ וְנָטְעוּ כְרָמִים וְשָׁתוּ
אֶת־יֵינָם וְעָשׂוּ גַנּוֹת וְאָכְלוּ אֶת־פְּרִיהֶם

"And I will turn the captivity of My people Israel,
And they shall build the waste cities, and inhabit them;
And they shall plant vineyards, and drink the wine thereof;
They shall also make gardens, and eat the fruit of them."
Amos 9:14

T he phrase "and they shall plant vineyards and
drink their wine" (ESV) is used by the prophet
Amos to describe what God plans to do as the
Israelites return to their land after years in exile. In

the Hebrew language used by Amos, the imagery is beautiful and meaningful.

In the first lines of Amos 9:14, God says, "And I will restore the fortunes of my people Israel, and they shall rebuild the ruined cities and inhabit them" (ESV). This is followed by the reference to vineyards and wine. The idea of planting vineyards and then drinking their wine, in the Hebrew language, implies that the Israelites will have a secure period of prosperity. However, this view barely scrapes the surface of the phrase's rich meaning.

Looking back at Amos 4, we read about numerous ways God is punishing the people of Israel for refusing to return to him (verse 6), despite all his efforts. An important verse for our discussion is Amos 4:9, which says, "I struck you with blight and mildew; your many gardens and your vineyards, your fig trees and your olive trees the locust devoured; yet you did not return to me" (ESV). In other words, we see that God sends locusts to devour the vineyards of Israel in hopes that they will return to him. Therefore, when God returns Israel to the land, as portrayed in Amos 9:14, the rich significance of the restored vineyards becomes more evident.

This is further clarified by a passage from Ezekiel with the same

wənaṭʿû kərāmîm wəšāṯû ʾeṯ yênām

וְנָטְעוּ כְרָמִים וְשָׁתוּ אֶת יֵינָם

"and they shall plant vineyards and drink their wine"

The people of Israel will plant vineyards and drink wine
—Amos 9:14

They shall dwell securely
—Ezekiel 28:25–26

They shall return to God and remain with him
—Isaiah 65:21–22

phrase, context, and imagery. In Ezekiel 28:25–26, God says, "I [will] gather the house of Israel from the peoples among whom they are scattered, and . . . then they shall dwell securely in it, and they shall build houses and plant vineyards. They shall dwell securely, when I execute judgments upon all their neighbors who have treated them with contempt. Then they will know that I am the LORD their God" (ESV).

This can be seen as an elegant distillation of what these vineyards symbolize. We are given a vision of God granting the Israelites vineyards and destroying their enemies, and these events convey to them that God is their God, and that there is no other.

The image of planting vineyards and reaping the fruit also connects to a well-known image in Isaiah 65:25: " 'The wolf and the lamb shall graze together; the lion shall eat straw like the ox, and dust shall be the serpent's food. They shall not hurt or destroy in all my holy mountain,' says the LORD" (ESV).

This compelling image, which many believe is a portrayal of the world to come, is preceded in verses 21–22 by poetic descriptions of planting vineyards and reaping abundant fruit. This vineyard imagery possibly implies that security, peace, and prosperity are the fruits of walking humbly with God.

וְנָטְעוּ
כְרָמִים וְשָׁתוּ
אֶת יֵינָם

וְשַׁבְתִּי

אֶת־שְׁבוּת

wəšabtî ʾet-šəbût

I will bring back those that . . .

wəšaḇtî ʾeṯ-šəḇûṯ -
וְשַׁבְתִּי אֶת־שְׁבוּת

שִׁיר הַמַּעֲלוֹת בְּשׁוּב יְהוָה אֶת־שִׁיבַת צִיּוֹן הָיִינוּ כְּחֹלְמִים

"When the LORD brought back those that returned to Zion, we were like unto them that dream."

Psalm 126:1

A story of tragic loss followed by amazing restoration is expressed in Jeremiah's letter to the Babylonian exiles. Jeremiah 29:14 says, "And I will be found of you, saith the LORD, and I will turn your captivity, and gather you from all the nations, and from all the places whither I have driven you, saith the LORD; and I will bring you back unto the place whence I caused you to be carried away captive."

The Hebrew phrase *wəšaḇtî ʾeṯ-šəḇûṯ* וְשַׁבְתִּי אֶת־שְׁבוּת ("I will bring back those that . . ." or "turn your captivity") exists in both Psalm 126:1 and Jeremiah 29:14. The Hebrew *wəšabtî* can be translated as "return" or "restore." The word *šəbût* refers to "captives" (*šəbî*) or people who repent (*təšûbāh* means "repentance"). *Šəbût* can also refer to something that a person deserves to get back, which in Jeremiah refers to an original state of government.

wəšabtî ʾet̠-šəbût̠

וְשַׁבְתִּי אֶת־שְׁבוּת

"I will bring back those that . . ."

Return the returnees
—Psalm 126:1

Return your captivity
—Jeremiah 29:14

Return to previous status
—Job 42:10

In the books of Job and Ezekiel, similar phrases refer to people who cannot be considered "captives" in any usual sense. In the King James Version, Job 42:10 says, "And the LORD turned the captivity of Job, when he prayed for his friends: also the LORD gave Job twice as much as he had before." In the story of Job, Job lost family, friends, livestock, property, and wealth, but he was never a captive. The King James Version of Ezekiel 16:53 also uses the terms "captive" and "captivity" for people in Sodom who were never held captive in the traditional sense of the word.

From these unusual translations, it's possible that the word *šəbût* is an expression of something lost, not necessarily related to the concept of captivity. Based on this interpretation of *šəbût*, these verses convey that something is missing and then restored to where it belongs. In other words, the Israelites are seen as missing (lost) from their land and then returned.

This view helps us better understand Psalm 126:1–2: "When the LORD brought back those that returned [or "were lost"] to Zion, we were like unto them that dream. Then our mouth was filled with laughter, and our tongue with singing; then said they among the nations: 'The LORD hath done great things with us; we are rejoiced.' "

Seen in this way, the psalm depicts the joy of a homecoming. Those who have been lost are now home.

וְשַׁבְתִּי
אֶת־שְׁבוּת

יָרֵשׁ

yāraš

to inherit

yāraš - יָרַשׁ

רְאֵה נָתַתִּי לִפְנֵיכֶם אֶת־הָאָרֶץ בֹּאוּ
וּרְשׁוּ אֶת־הָאָרֶץ אֲשֶׁר נִשְׁבַּע יְהוָה
לַאֲבֹתֵיכֶם לְאַבְרָהָם לְיִצְחָק וּלְיַעֲקֹב
לָתֵת לָהֶם וּלְזַרְעָם אַחֲרֵיהֶם

"Behold, I have set the land before you: go in and possess the land
which the LORD swore unto your fathers, to Abraham, to Isaac,
and to Jacob, to give unto them and to their seed after them."

Deuteronomy 1:8

King David, writing in Psalm 24:1–2, reminds his readers that God is the creator and ultimate owner of all things: "The earth is the LORD's, and the fullness thereof; the world, and they that dwell therein. For He hath founded it upon the seas, and established it upon the floods."

Based on these verses, many people believe that life and breath, and the material world in which we live, is not earned but given to humanity. So, perhaps it is best to see life as an inheritance. And that is what the Hebrew word *yāraš* conveys: life is an inheritance that God wants people to receive.

The idea of *yāraš*, or "to inherit," appears early in the Hebrew Bible. In Genesis 12, God tells Abram (later called Abraham) to leave his region and his home and go to an undisclosed land. God also promises that he will make Abram a blessing to all the families of the earth (Genesis 12:1–3).

God leads Abram to the land of Canaan, but he does not let Abram take possession of the land (Genesis 12:6). Instead, God makes another promise to Abram: "To your offspring I will give this land" (Genesis 12:7, ESV). In this verse, God asks Abram to live on the basis of a promise, without a land to call his own.

Much later, after Moses leads the Israelites out of slavery in Egypt, God initiates the process of giving Canaan to Abraham's offspring. In Deuteronomy 1:8, God says to Moses, "See, I have set the land before you. Go in and take possession [*yāraš*] of the land that the LORD swore to your fathers, to Abraham, to Isaac, and to Jacob, to give to them and to their offspring after them" (ESV). This verse uses וּרְשׁוּ, which is a conjugated form of *yāraš*.

yāraš

יָרַשׁ

"to inherit"

Receive/Possess an inheritance on behalf of the father
—Deuteronomy 1:8

Be granted by God
—Genesis 15:7–8

Guided prosperously by God
—Ezekiel 36:12

This usage emphasizes the idea of taking possession, but it includes the notion that the land is an inheritance. In other words, we can reasonably conclude that God is giving the Israelites a gift ("inheritance") *and* that they are to receive it ("take possession").

Perhaps the word *yāraš* can offer fresh insights for our modern lives. In a meritocracy, people often emphasize the importance of "taking possession" of wealth and property through hard work alone. Work is valued in the Bible (Genesis 1:28, 2:15). But, what about the other connotation of *yāraš*, the idea of receiving an inheritance? What is the proper response to receiving what has been given to us in life?

In the book of Leviticus, the Israelites offer sacrifices of thanksgiving (Leviticus 7:12–15). Nehemiah, in completing the reconstruction of the wall around Jerusalem, brings all the Levites to the city "to celebrate the dedication with gladness, with thanksgivings and with singing, with cymbals, harps, and lyres" (Nehemiah 12:27, ESV). Numerous psalms remind God's people to be thankful and joyful for all of God's gifts. "Let us come into his presence with thanksgiving; let us make a joyful noise to him with songs of praise!" (Psalm 95:2, ESV).

יָרַשׁ

zēḵer

a memory

zēk̲er - זֵכֶר

שִׁבְעַת יָמִים תֹּאכַל־עָלָיו מַצּוֹת לְמַעַן
תִּזְכֹּר אֶת־יוֹם צֵאתְךָ מֵאֶרֶץ מִצְרַיִם כֹּל
יְמֵי חַיֶּיךָ

*"Seven days shalt thou eat unleavened bread therewith . . . that
thou mayest remember the day when thou camest forth out of the
land of Egypt all the days of thy life."*
Deuteronomy 16:3

The Bible contains many exhortations to the people of Israel to remember the past and to pass stories on to the next generations. For example, in Deuteronomy 16:3, God tells his people to set aside the Passover week to remember the exodus from Egypt. The Passover tradition of eating unleavened bread, which represents affliction, is designed to help people remember the haste with which the Israelites escaped slavery under Pharaoh. Jewish people believe that by adhering to Passover traditions, they are better able to reinforce their shared identity and to transmit that identity to future generations.

In Hebrew, the word for "a memory" is *zēker* (זֵכֶר). When *zēker* is attached to a biblical remembrance, it takes on the idea of "a pointer," something prominent that captures our attention to help us remember. In English, we might call this a mnemonic device, or a reminder. Memorials in the Bible, such as the Passover, point back to an event that is central to Jewish history and identity.

Deuteronomy 25 provides another example of when God instructs his people to recall a significant event in their history. He tells them to never forget what the evil nation of Amalek did to them as they escaped from Egypt:

> *"Remember what Amalek did to you on the way as you came out of Egypt, how he attacked you on the way when you were faint and weary, and cut off your tail, those who were lagging behind you, and he did not fear God. Therefore when the LORD your God has given you rest from all your enemies around you, in the land that the LORD your God is giving you for an inheritance to possess, you shall blot out the memory of Amalek from under heaven; you shall not forget" (verses 17–19, ESV).*

zēker

זֵכֶר

"a memory"

Remember forever
—Deuteronomy 16:3

Remember and never forget
—Deuteronomy 25:17–19

Keep on your mind
—Psalm 77:12–13

In Psalm 77:12–13, the psalmist writes: "I will make mention of the deeds of the LORD; yea, I will remember Thy wonders of old. I will meditate also upon all Thy work, and muse on Thy doings." And in Psalm 78:4, the psalmist emphasizes the importance of passing history on to children: "We will not hide from their children, telling to the generation to come the praises of the LORD, and His strength, and His wondrous works that He hath done."

Perhaps these Bible passages can help us elevate the importance of remembering significant events in our own lives. The commandment of God in Deuteronomy 16:3 calls the people of Israel to be intentional about maintaining their history. This implies that to remember something is to acknowledge its weight, significance, and relevance.

זָכַר

זֶבַח

zeḇaḥ

a sacrifice

zebaḥ - זֶבַח

לֹא־תִזְבַּח לַיהוָה אֱלֹהֶיךָ שׁוֹר וָשֶׂה אֲשֶׁר יִהְיֶה בוֹ מוּם כֹּל דָּבָר רָע כִּי תוֹעֲבַת יְהוָה אֱלֹהֶיךָ הוּא

"Thou shalt not sacrifice unto the LORD thy God an ox, or a sheep, wherein is a blemish, even any evil thing; for that is an abomination unto the LORD thy God."

Deuteronomy 17:1

God gives a straightforward command to the people of Israel in Leviticus 19:18: "You shall love your neighbor as yourself" (ESV). To live out this command requires a person to at times sacrifice their own self-interests in order to better love and serve others. In our lives, we often make sacrifices in our relationships with the people closest to us.

However, the biblical concept of *sacrifice* can be better understood by studying the Hebrew word *zebaḥ* (זֶבַח), which usually refers to physical sacrifices. The Bible uses this

Hebrew term to describe many types of sacrifices, often seen as ways of reaching out to God, seeking atonement and forgiveness of sins (Leviticus 4:26), or offering thanksgiving (Leviticus 7).

In the Hebrew Bible, the people of Israel offer sacrifices for two primary purposes: for sins and in relation to the Passover. With the sin offering, an animal is sacrificed so that the person can live. The purpose is to bring about the reconciliation between a sinful person and a holy God. In order to be acceptable to God, the sacrifices had to follow the exact specifications required by God. The animal presented as a sacrifice described in Deuteronomy 17:1, for example, could not contain any blemishes.

We see another example of God's specific requirements for a sacrifice with the Passover lamb just before the Israelites escape from Egypt. Lambs were sacrificed by the Israelites in Egypt in order to prevent their firstborn sons from being killed during the final plague on the Egyptians. God tells the Israelites:

"Your lamb shall be without blemish, a male a year old. You may take it from the sheep or from the goats, and you shall keep it until the fourteenth day of this month, when the whole assembly of the congregation of Israel shall kill their lambs at twilight.

zebaḥ

זֶבַח

"a sacrifice"

Sacrifice as a meal
—Genesis 31:54

Sacrifice as an offering to God
—1 Kings 8:63

Slaughter by God's judgment
—Ezekiel 39:17–19

"Then they shall take some of the blood and put it on the two doorposts and the lintel of the houses in which they eat it. They shall eat the flesh that night, roasted on the fire; with unleavened bread and bitter herbs they shall eat it. . . . And you shall eat it in haste. It is the LORD's Passover. For I will pass through the land of Egypt that night, and I will strike all the firstborn in the land of Egypt, both man and beast; and on all the gods of Egypt I will execute judgments: I am the LORD. The blood shall be a sign for you, on the houses where you are. And when I see the blood, I will pass over you, and no plague will befall you to destroy you, when I strike the land of Egypt." (Exodus 12:5–13, ESV)

In the story in Exodus 12, God responds to the people's obedience by protecting their lives. In other Bible references to sacrifices, God responds to the people's obedience by offering them forgiveness for their sin (Leviticus 4:35). Through these biblical accounts, it's possible to see that for the people of Israel, a sacrifice (*zebaḥ*) is about obedience to God—not necessarily about the sacrifice itself. We can perhaps conclude that the act of obedience through the offering of the sacrifice probably strengthened the relationship between the people and God.

Similarly, our tasks of sacrificial service each day can more deeply connect us to those we love and serve.

זֶבַח

Notes

1. Rashi, commentary on Deuteronomy 6:5, Sefaria.org, http://www.sefaria.org/Rashi_on_Deuteronomy.6.5.2?lang=bi.

2. Rabbi Eliyahu Dessler, "Kuntres Hachesed," Michtav M'Eliyahu, vol. 1 (early 1900s).

3. This passage is listed as Exodus 22:22–24 in some translations of the Bible.

4. Ramban (Nachmanides): Commentary on the Torah (5 vol. set) (New York: Judaica Press, 2005).

5. This passage is listed as Hosea 2:18 in some translations of the Bible.

6. Rashi, commentary on Psalm 89:28.

7. Abraham Ben Meir Ibn Ezra and H. Norman Strickman, Ibn Ezra's Commentary on the Pentateuch: Leviticus, vol. 3 (New York: Menorah Publishing, 2004).

8. Annie Dillard, *For the Time Being* (New York: Alfred Knopf, 1999), 196–197.

9. Judah HaLevi, The Kuzari (Santa Fe, NM: Gaon Books, 2015).

museum of the Bible

Experience the Book
That Shapes History

Museum of the Bible is a 430,000-square-foot building located in the heart of Washington, DC—just steps from the National Mall and the U.S. Capitol. Displaying artifacts from several collections, the Museum explores the Bible's history, narrative and impact through high-tech exhibits, immersive settings, and interactive experiences. Upon entering, you will pass through two massive, bronze gates resembling printing plates from Genesis 1. Beyond the gates, an incredible replica of an ancient artifact containing Psalm 19 hangs behind etched glass panels. Come be inspired by the imagination and innovation used to display thousands of years of biblical history.

Museum of the Bible aims to be the most technologically advanced museum in the world, starting with its unique Digital Guide that allows guests to personalize their museum experience with navigation, customized tours, supplemental visual and audio content, and more.

For more information and to plan your visit, go to
museumoftheBible.org.